"Bill Newlin has written a compulsively readable book about his unknown career in the State Department as a secret, solitary drinker. As an undergraduate at Harvard, he had already mastered the skills of a high-functioning alcoholic, which, after graduation, allowed him to rise through the ranks of the Foreign Service but prevented him from always making the grade as a husband and father. A must-read for anyone with alcohol as a family member."

—Barbara Meade, co-founder of
Politics and Prose, Washington DC

"Riveting, insightful and honest, this book examines a life long shaped by secrecy and addiction. It is an artful and courageous tale. It is also a love story for Bill Newlin's steadfast wife Louisa and for readers who will recognize themselves and find inspiration in his ultimately redemptive story."

—Frances Stead Sellers,
senior writer for *The Washington Post*

"On many levels, *Drunk at the State Department* is a compelling and absorbing book. It is, first of all, the account of one individual's battle with alcoholism, through all t...

familiar stages of delusion and denial, until finally coming to grips with it. It is also a fascinating description of being an alcoholic within the confines of the Foreign Service. One marvels at how well William Newlin managed to function despite the alcoholism and how long his problems went undetected—or did his colleagues and superiors just choose to ignore them? The Foreign Service does not have a brilliant record of dealing with alcoholism in its ranks, though it has surely improved them since the 1960s. Mr. Newlin is to be commended for his courage in this frank telling of his story."

—AVIS BOHLEN,
FORMER U.S. AMBASSADOR TO BULGARIA

"William Newlin has written an honest account of his addiction to alcohol that began when he was in his teens and continued through Harvard and Harvard Business School, his 28 years as a Foreign Service Officer, and for a time thereafter. He describes his dependency in eloquent prose, makes no excuses, and blames no one but himself. This is a compelling and thought-provoking read."

—JAMES G. LOWENSTEIN,
FORMER U.S. AMBASSADOR TO LUXEMBOURG

"Be prepared for the rousing good time the title suggests, and the best of it is that you'll wake up the next morning with no hangover and the startling conviction you've hung out with a deeply engaging storyteller. Bill Newlin is the master of the all-telling detail and has written a classic in the literary realm of alcohol."

—TOM DOWLING, FORMER BOOK EDITOR
FOR *THE SAN FRANCISCO EXAMINER*

Four Winds Press
San Francisco, CA

print ISBN: 978-1-940423-14-2
ebook ISBN: 978-1-940423-15-9

Cover and interior design by Domini Dragoone
Cover photos: Tom Kelley Archive/iStock, South Agency/iStock

9  8  7  6  5  4  3  2  1

Distributed by Publishers Group West

# DRUNK AT THE
# STATE DEPARTMENT

FOR LOUISA

# TABLE OF CONTENTS

# DRUNK AT THE

# STATE DEPARTMENT

## A MEMOIR

WILLIAM V. P. NEWLIN

**FOUR WINDS**
— PRESS —

SAN FRANCISCO

MEMOIR

# 1

## RESPECTING THE COCKTAIL HOUR

*Between the dark and the daylight,*
*When the night is beginning to lower,*
*Comes a pause in the day's occupations,*
*That is known as the Children's Hour.*

—HENRY WADSWORTH LONGFELLOW

DURING MY CHILDHOOD, LONGFELLOW'S VICTORIAN poem, "The Children's Hour" was better known to me with a waggish twist: There is "a pause in the day's occupations … known as the cocktail hour." The cocktail hour figures prominently in my earliest memories. It was a year-round phenomenon, with the large stone fireplace in our house dominating my recollections. Dad is home from the office, and in colder months we are all gathered in front of a cheery blaze, large logs set on heavy andirons.

I am unclear at what age we children got to participate regularly in the nightly cocktail ritual—probably earlier than I recall. When the three of us were small, one of our nanny's primary duties was to keep my older brother, younger sister, and me out from underfoot at inconvenient times such as the cocktail hour and dinner time. My earliest memory of being present at "cocktails" was as a guest, not a regular. I remember being paraded in, already bathed and ready for bed, in jammies—with attached feet for the youngest—and a robe. What sticks with me to this day is the welcoming atmosphere of that cozy, relaxed, and civilized family gathering. I still see Mother on the couch, Dad in his chair. Smiles, good cheer, pleasant aromas—the fire and Mother's perfume. No problems anywhere.

My parents' drink of choice then was the old-fashioned, which was really just a tarted-up version of a whiskey on the rocks. The classic old-fashioned then was made with rye, a whiskey which was demoted to describe cheap bar whiskey—as in "give me a rye and ginger." It went out of style for years, but may be making a comeback.

Old-fashioneds were made in "rocks" glasses—then widely called old-fashioned glasses. Start with a few dashes of Angostura bitters on a square cube of sugar and add a jigger of rye. (In our family, we measured.) Next, crush the sugar cube, using a short glass swizzle stick, with a small round, flat end designed just for that purpose. Stir until the sugar is dissolved. Then add a freshly cut twist of lemon and fill the glass with crushed ice. Top it off with a few drops of water from a small silver pitcher and crown the whole thing with a maraschino cherry. Voilà.

The details of the composition of that drink come not from my memory as a toddler with booties on my pj's, but from later, when I was ten or so. Then I was sometimes given the heady responsibility of preparing the old-fashioneds myself. I sometimes asked for the privilege, but some evenings, Dad, normally the drinks maker, just felt like sitting in front of the fire and having his drink brought to him. I was always pleased to be asked to do the honors and was proud of making the old-fashioneds just right. From my perspective, my parents were both moderate drinkers back then. Each drink contained its measured jigger of whiskey—one and a half ounces. This was invariably followed by a "dividend"—an ounce for Mother and another ounce and a half for Dad. This drill was repeated, night after night.

I have indulged in this rather long digression about the old-fashioned because it was my introduction to alcohol, and I want to describe the context in which I had my first taste of that odd, bittersweet drink. I don't know how old I was, but not very. I remember clearly being invited to dip my finger into the exotic, grown-up concoction and being encouraged to taste it. And I remember my reaction. Sweet as it was, and pretty with its red cherry, I grimaced. I recoiled from its strong, pungent taste. Still, I knew even then that I should like it. Grownups did. Mother and Father did. Even then, I wanted to like it, too. It took me years to develop a taste for whiskey, and in my teens, I forced myself to drink it way before I had learned to like it. I knew it played a big part in the world I wanted to enter, so learn to like it I did. But I don't want to get too far ahead of myself.

When I was growing up, we lived in three different houses, undergoing two moves in the process. What was unusual was that all three houses were on contiguous properties, so each move was only to the house next door. Each new house was a bit bigger and more grand than the last. In each, however, the bar setup was always identical. The bar was a freestanding wooden affair designed for that one purpose. This odd piece of furniture was ubiquitous in the forties and fifties in the houses of our friends and relations, but they appear to have since disappeared; I haven't seen one in ages. They stood about waist-high, with a spill-proof surface of about two feet by three, with a second shelf underneath. A rail around the sides and back kept things from falling off. It was a simple dry bar: no water, no drain.

The bar was in a prominent place, usually in the living room, and it was not just brought out for guests but was, like the other furniture, in its place day and night. On it were all the makings of most drinks that might be called for. Although Mother and Dad could be counted on to have their old-fashioneds, guests' requests could be unpredictable, so there had to be an inclusive selection: at least the three whiskeys—rye, bourbon, scotch—plus gin and rum, and sherry and vermouth. I think vodka came later. No beer or wine. My parents and their friends did not drink beer, and wine was not yet widely drunk as an aperitif in their circles. The usual mixers like club soda and ginger ale and a small assortment of esoteric, little or never-used bottles to accompany the Angostura bitters completed the picture. A lower shelf held fortified wines like sherry, port, and brandy and liqueurs like Cointreau and crème de menthe, which were only trotted out for dinner parties.

A small assortment of glasses were permanent fixtures on the bar, but every evening at the appointed time, the right number of the right-sized glasses, a filled ice bucket, the aforementioned small pitcher of water and a plate of hors d'oeuvres—often just crackers and cheese—appeared. In the early days, we had just one maid and the governess, with only the latter in residence. Then it was Mother who set up the bar for the cocktail hour. Later, when there was a succession of live-in couples to help in my parents' house, it was the man's job to stock the bar.

This whole cocktail drill was an established part of our family's routine, a prescribed dance like a minuet, in which the few nightly or seasonal variations did not challenge, but rather confirmed, the form. It is one that my wife Louisa and I incorporated into the early years of our own marriage—minus the household help. I, especially, considered the cocktail hour of my youth to be, like well-ordered meals with the right plates and cutlery, a reliable outward sign of a civilized existence. If you kept up those routines, you were on the right track for a well-ordered life.

# 2

## BEING BAD
## AT BAR HARBOR

AS I CHRONICLE THIS ACCOUNT OF ALCOHOL'S ROLE in my life, it should be clear that while it played a ritualistic role in the household of my childhood, I can't lay my own later problems on my parents. I grew up uneventfully in a leafy Philadelphia Main Line suburb. I was eight on December 7, 1941, though the war barely touched my family. My father limped from shrapnel wounds received in France in 1917, but he and all the uncles on both sides, having fought in that one, were too old for this second conflict. All the war meant to me and my siblings—Frank, who was two years older than me, and Lucy Bell, two years younger—was gas rationing, coupons for butter, meat, and shoes, and little balls of saved tinfoil.

We drove to Beach Haven on the New Jersey shore for summer vacation until I was about nine, and then to Pocono Lake Preserve in the Pocono Mountains of Pennsylvania. At the beach, we played in the sand, caught crabs, and began to learn to sail cat boats on the bay. At Pocono Lake Preserve, we paddled canoes, fished, and actually raced sailboats. The closest thing to lost innocence in those years were my twelve-year-old dreams of taking my true love, with long hair the color of an Irish setter, paddling in a canoe by moonlight. But first, I had to get up the nerve to talk to her—which I never did.

I was thirteen when we first went to Northeast Harbor on Mount Desert Island, Maine. Northeast Harbor was called "Philadelphia on the Rocks" by the in-group—which might have served as a red flag. It was on that idyllic island that alcohol began to play a role in my own life. Having an older brother, Frank, who was sixteen, certainly helped get me started. He and all his friends were beginning to drink. Being known to have drunk a whole six-pack of beer or having "gotten loaded" brought cachet in that set. I wanted that cachet.

My memory is imperfect and I don't remember my very first illicit drinks, except that the drink of choice was beer and I could barely get it down. One of my first youthful drinking exploits surrounds a three-day cruise sponsored by the local yacht club that was known as The

Fleet. Sailboat racing was a big deal in Northeast Harbor, and there was a large racing fleet which included three classes of knockabouts, all roughly thirty feet long with small cabins and no auxiliary motors. Dad had chartered an "A Boat," one of the most popular classes, a lovely gaff-rigged sloop with graceful lines. They raced twice a week for July and August series cups, and in each month there was a three-day cruise involving races to nearby harbors. The July Cruise was scheduled for shortly after our arrival that first year and Dad was delighted. That was just the sort of thing he thought we had come for. Frank, of course, was the skipper. Dave, his roommate at St. Paul's School, was the first mate. I was the boy. "Not bad for two men and a boy," Dave would say when we did well in a race.

From the beginning, even though we were brand-new to the community and had never been on one of the cruises, we boys knew drinking was a big part of the cruise culture; word got around. Of course, we were not old enough to drink with permission, but we weren't going to let that slow us down. The first trick was figuring out how to get a three-day supply of beer on board without my parents knowing. These knockabouts are not cruising boats. The cabins are just large enough to get you out of the weather and to put a couple of sleeping bags in for sleeping rough, not a place to stash a couple of cases of beer out of sight of your parents, who you know are going to want to participate, if only on the fringes, in the provisioning effort.

One design feature that made an A boat so graceful was its overhung stern and transom. A safety feature of the boat was that the area of dead space in the stern was sealed off so if you capsized, air would be caught back there and you wouldn't sink. That was the theory, at least. In all the years I have sailed A boats, I have never known one to founder for long enough to discover whether it would have sunk. Some motor launch has always come to the rescue. But whatever its merits as a safety measure, that empty space was a perfect place to stow large quantities of beer. The only access to it was a brass fitting about eight inches in diameter in the deck in the middle of the overhung stern. Down that hole, under cover of darkness two nights before our departure, can by can went a case of Miller High Life, and another of Pabst Blue Ribbon. When Mother came aboard to admire all our preparations for the grand adventure, as we had been sure she would, we had no fear at all that our cache would be discovered.

Having all that beer was great for Frank and Dave. It gave them more than they could ever drink themselves and made our boat very popular with the rest of their less foresighted buddies. In fact, there was even some left when we all limped back to home port three days later. Having all that beer had been a problem for me, however. I wanted to be one of the guys too, a beer drinker. But I could barely get it down. I had to insist first on getting my share, and then to get rid of it surreptitiously. It was easy enough taking big fake swigs; the trick was pouring overboard what I was pretending to drink without being seen. I think by the end of the cruise Frank was on to me, but if he was, we had so much beer he didn't really care, and he didn't rat me out to Dave.

By the time the August cruise came around, we were minor celebrities and word got around the fleet as to where to store beer on A boats, so we never had to take as much again. Moreover, I had learned, if not to like it, at least to drink my share. I was never quite the same again.

That was also the summer I learned the hard way the difference between the effects of hard liquor and beer. The summer colony in Northeast Harbor had a well-developed sense of noblesse oblige, and one of the ways this manifested itself had been the construction by the summer colony, well before my time, of a substantial "Neighborhood House" with a large auditorium for the use of the town. It had many uses, one of which was to host a late-summer variety show put on by the summer youth.

I am hazy about who organized it, but the summer I was fourteen I was absolutely thrilled to be asked to participate in two skits being staged by much older boys, Mike Peabody and Bump Hadley. They must have been seventeen or eighteen, even older than Frank (who didn't do variety shows). Our numbers involved both song and dance. In the first, the three of us would play fishermen in yellow slickers and sou'wester hats dancing around a pile of lobster traps, singing an old sea shanty whose refrain went, "A porpoise and a porgy and the other was me." In the other, I was to dance around, loose-jointed, as we all sang "Dem bones, dem bones going to jump around," etc.

It became clear enough early in rehearsal that I had been hired as the loose-jointed dancer, but I was also expected to pull my weight in the song department—which I couldn't do. So I had to suffer the humiliation of having my roles cut little by little to reduce my part in the singing. In spite of this, however, I was happy. I had a real part in two skits involving the older set, which put me in close contact with the older girls, such as the beauteous Lee twins, Devie Hunter, and Ellen Van Pelt. Even at fourteen, I was old enough to flirt. Happily, they humored the youngster trying so hard to play with the big boys—and girls.

The show—a great success, by all accounts—was followed by a cast party at someone's big, gracious house. I still hadn't started to really like beer, but I certainly was going to insist on my share in that august company. The girls had other ideas. They introduced me to a punch they were drinking called Purple Jesus, gin and grape juice, obviously a concoction of tremendous sophistication. The key details surrounding that evening are no longer clear. I remember great gaiety, merriment and song, and high hilarity. I remember thinking how good Purple Jesus was. To what extent anyone actually tried to get me drunk, or to what extent I did it all by myself, I'll never know. The end of the party and my trip home is lost. I made it down the difficult driveway and to my bedroom without waking anyone, but my later violent retching and vomiting in my bed woke my mother, who came to my aid—more in sorrow than in anger. She got me clean pajamas, stripped the bed—an unholy mess of purple vomit—and remade it while I changed.

She didn't say much that night. I really wasn't in any condition to listen, let alone respond; but she didn't say much in the morning either. Her line wasn't so much that I had done something wrong as that I had made a mistake. I had miscalculated how much punch I could drink. It was an understandable youthful error. Cast parties are notorious, and punch is a killer—it sneaks up on you. The unspoken conviction was that it had been a learning experience. I don't remember Dad's ever acknowledging anything at all about the incident; it is even possible that he didn't know about it.

It was some time before I could stomach even the smell of gin, but by the next summer I had graduated to a new level of sophistication—Tom Collinses at the Bar Harbor Club. That was enough to dispel my aversion to the taste of gin. The taste of grape juice, however, even its smell, made me feel sick for years; I still don't drink it.

The summer of 1948 was a milestone for me; I had turned fifteen. In Pennsylvania, where most of my friends and I lived, you couldn't get a driver's license until you were sixteen, but in Maine, fifteen-year-olds could drive. I suppose farmers in the big rural counties upstate wanted their kids to be able to help out by driving the pickup trucks on the local roads. Happily, fifteen-year-old out-of-staters, just in Maine for vacation, could get licenses, too.

Dad thought driving was a good thing to teach a young man responsibility, so he was happy to teach me to drive the stick-shift Willys American, which he bought to get the most miles possible from our "C" gas ration card, the lowest level. Our pre-war car, which we kept for the duration but didn't use much, was a big gas-guzzling La Salle. (It had a wide running board on which we kids were sometimes allowed to ride for the length of our grandmother's mile-long driveway at "the Farm.") The little Willys was a cheap, tinny affair which we called the "Jeep," because Willys also made that famous Army war horse. I loved it and always will—it was the car I learned to drive in.

Dad was a wonderful man and father in so many ways, but an impatient teacher. He thought to say a thing was to teach it; if the pupil didn't get it the first time, he just had to say it more forcefully and more often. But the intricacies of the four-speed stick shift were not beyond me, even with Dad as my guide, and by early July I was mobile. As a driver, I could run with the big boys. (The miracle is that we didn't all die on the road to Bar Harbor or its equivalent. Many did.)

Northeast Harbor, then as now, was pretty innocent as resorts go. In marked contrast to many classy resorts, where drinking was a big part of the fun at the tennis, sailing, swimming, and golf clubs, none of the clubs in Northeast and Seal Harbors served any alcohol at all—and interestingly, surprisingly, the no-booze-in-the-clubs rule worked. There was very little daytime drinking. And as there were no bars or nightspots, there wasn't a lot of evening drinking—outside of private homes—except at the Bar Harbor Club.

Northeast Harbor's summer community focused on the simple life from its beginnings. The founding of the Northeast Harbor summer colony was spearheaded by the likes of Bishop William Doane of Albany, President Charles Eliot of Harvard, and other lesser but no less cerebral lights. Those early summer visitors were dubbed "rusticators." High life took a back seat. Neighboring Seal Harbor was strongly influenced by its greatest patron, John D. Rockefeller, whose family was famous for its abstemious habits. Hence the dry clubs.

Bar Harbor, on the other hand, was vying to be the next Newport. The many vast "cottages" of the likes of the New York Atwater Kents and the Chicago Potter Palmers had marble ballrooms and crystal chandeliers. The Bar Harbor

Club reflected this difference among the various communities. Even in the daytime, the Bar Harbor Club's bar vied
with its tennis courts and pool as the center of attention. In
the evening, there was no contest; the bar ruled.

On Mount Desert Island, the round of festivities
included no fewer than four weekly dances, each with live
music produced by the orchestra of Harry Marshard of Boston. On the abstemious Northeast Harbor side of the island,
it was the Kimball House, a great white frame, turn-of-the-
century, wedding cake of a hotel that hosted the weekly
dance on Monday. It attracted a young crowd—early to
mid-teens. My recollection is that by about eighteen, the
smart set had better things to do. But for the younger set,
on Monday, the Kimball House dance was the place to be.
The dance floor was ringed by a large covered porch with
rocking chairs, in which the nosy elderly ladies of the summer community took up their positions, the better to act as
unofficial chaperones of the proceedings. But chaperoning
wasn't in much need. Even the bad boys—among whom
I liked to number myself—didn't smuggle booze to those
dances or sneak away to hidden stashes. They were what
they were meant to be: innocent diversions. My first overt
act in my courtship of my future wife Louisa was to walk her
home after a Kimball House dance. I didn't even kiss her.

The dances at Seal Harbor were even more innocent.
They took place on Thursday evenings and were dinner

dances, because Thursday, for this upper-crust set, was "maid's night out." The teen—and even pre-teen—set attended these affairs, but *en famille*. The little ones danced with their daddies. The Bunny Hop was the *pièce de résistance*. Not a drop of booze to be seen.

But Tuesday and Saturday nights belonged to the Bar Harbor Club. In the late forties and early fifties, ladies and gentlemen wore "black tie"—dinner jacket—more than is the current custom. Saturday night was black tie. Tuesday, you could get by with a blue blazer and a four-in-hand, but most of the older set wore black tie anyway. By the time I was sixteen or seventeen, those dances had become the center of my summer life. They eclipsed the tennis; they eclipsed the sailing, the mountains, and the fishing. They were the part of the week I looked forward to most. How could that be? What was it about those dances that gave them such importance in my mind? The alcohol.

What did I do at the Bar Harbor Club for it to have marked me so? Nothing much that I can remember. Nothing remarkable. I was one of the youngest there. Even my eighteen-year-old brother and his friends were on the young side. Most of the participants were real grownups. Many of them were rich and not shy about showing it. The rather quiet folks in Northeast Harbor, and this glitzy Bar Harbor contingent, traveled in quite different circles and there was relatively little overlap. The

Dorrances, the Colkets, and the Waterfords were part of a different group than my parents.

An investment banker in his professional life, my dad was most happy during outdoor activities, like canoeing, fly fishing, or sailing. My mother was highly social and had many friends, but put more stock in her volunteer activities at the library and low-key socializing than in fancy clothes or keeping up appearances. There were people who dressed up twice a week to drink and dance at the Bar Harbor Club. It simply would not have occurred to my parents, or any of their friends, to do that.

The fact that none of my parents' friends ever appeared at these affairs may have been more important to my experience at the Bar Harbor Club than I realized. The late-teen, early-twenties gang knew me. They were my friends and allies. However, none of the older people knew me at all. I was invisible to anyone who might have raised an eyebrow at my behavior.

I hung around with my brother's friends and the few of my own age who were there. (As I got older, more of my contemporaries went.) I danced with such older girls who would have me. And I drank Tom Collinses. That's about the least sophisticated drink I can imagine now—lemonade and gin. It may have been unsophisticated then, too, but it was popular, even with the fancy adults, which is probably why I liked it—that, and it tasted just like lemonade.

I didn't even drink very many of them, or at least it seemed to me. For one thing, I couldn't afford to. Drinks cost seventy-five cents each and I felt I had to leave a buck. All the grown-ups did. But four, or maybe five was all I wanted or needed—especially since I jollied the bartenders to make me strong drinks. I certainly drank more than I should have, but I didn't get smashed. I just got high.

Looking back now, what I want to know is what came first? Was it the alcohol that drew me to the Bar Harbor Club every Tuesday and Saturday? Or was it being there with the big guys, being there and being a little bad, that drew me to the booze? Which was the chicken, which the egg? I always wanted to be a little bad. It was my image of myself—a little wild. Was that all from brother Frank? Or did I get it on my own?

Whatever I did, and whyever I did it, the Bar Harbor Club marked me. The Tuesday dances were over at midnight, the Saturday dances at one in the morning. I never wanted them to end. It was Billy Newlin who went around with the hat to pay the band when Harry Marshard started playing "Good Night Ladies," threatening to end the festivities. And I was pretty persuasive; it usually wouldn't take long to get the $150 needed for another hour. There were always a couple of grown-ups who wanted it to go on even more than I did. They were always good for a fifty.

## 3

# SEEKING COMFORT AT BOARDING SCHOOL

IN THE FALL OF 1947, AT THE AGE OF FOURTEEN, I was sent off to board at St. Paul's School in Concord, New Hampshire. Frank had preceded me there by two years and was well-established when I arrived. Drinking, of course, was an offense that merited expulsion—you could even get bounced for smoking—but to me the fact that booze was forbidden fruit just added to its allure.

In fact, at fourteen, that was the main allure. I had not yet developed even the beginning of a drinking habit, just a habit of breaking the rules—and at St. Paul's then, drinking was the biggest taboo around. The teenage world was largely drug free in 1947. The first few months, I was too busy to think much about drinking. Sports were big at St. Paul's, then—still are—and I was deep into football in the fall, and when winter came, ice hockey. Hockey was really big at St. Paul's. In fact, Christmas holidays started off with a hockey game in Madison Square Garden in New York—St. Paul's against one of the Ivy freshmen teams; SPS often won. So for the first few months, sports kept me out of trouble.

But in New England, you don't get spring as we do farther south. You get "slush season." There is a long, messy gap between the time when the ice on the pond becomes too soft for skating and when spring sports can start. The baseball diamonds and tracks are soggy and the lake is still icy, so rowing can't start, either. It's a time when the boys have time on their hands. "The devil finds work for idle hands." He found work for mine.

Frank had paved the way. The first hurdle was just getting the alcohol. Paulies stood out in Concord, so using the liquor stores, even if we hadn't been too young, would have been risky. But SPS students had first faced this problem years ago and had fixed on the time-honored solution—a bootlegger. A man named Cooley had been running a little cottage industry, supplying strong drink to renegade St. Paul's kids for ages. Frank briefed me.

Cooley lived in a little white frame house less than two miles from the school on the School Farm Road. He was well-situated, because walking out to the School

Farm Road was a "safe" route, the beginning of the "big circle" walk of about five miles. You just had to be sure you weren't spotted leaving the School Farm Road and heading up the lane that led through a wood to Cooley's innocent-looking abode.

I remember many details about my first foray into Mr. Cooley's domain. It was early Saturday afternoon, free time, nothing to do until supper. I was going to walk the aforementioned "big circle." That was my cover. But no one asked; no nosey parker saw me leave school, and I met no one on the road. Cooley's house was easy to find. After a careful look around, I turned off the safety of the School Farm Road and up Cooley's long drive. The woods around Cooley's house had been described to me as providing cover from the main road, and they would once the undergrowth leafed out in May, but there I was in March. The drive was exposed to prying eyes. As I marched up the whole 100 yards, I was trying to invent a plausible reason for a detour to that little white house if I were spotted.

"What's Newlin up to?" any master who saw me would wonder.

Once at the door, I was in a hurry to get inside—out of sight. I knocked. Nothing. I knocked again. I had no appointment. Even if I had had Cooley's number, I couldn't easily have used it. The only way boys could call out from St. Paul's was to go to the business office and get permission to use the telephone. Permission was reserved for emergencies.

My third knock was answered promptly by "Who's there?" from right inside the door. "Who's there?" needed an answer. Who was I? No name, for sure.

"I'm from the school," I said.

"Wait." I heard a latch being opened, and the door swung in. I was facing a scraggly-looking skinny guy in blue jean overalls, shaggy gray hair and gray stubble whiskers. "Come on in," he said, pleasantly enough. He didn't seem surprised to see an obvious Paulie at his door. I came in and went right to the point.

"They tell me you'll sell me a pint of whiskey," I said.

"They're right," he said. "I'll do that. Ten bucks." Without another word, he turned and disappeared through a door to the back of the house. In less than a minute, he was back.

He took the ten bucks, I took the brown paper bag he was clutching. The whole thing was over in less time than it takes to tell, and I was out on the front stoop with my pint of Four Roses in its brown paper bag, with the door shut firmly behind me. I felt even more exposed as I hurried back to the safety of the big circle route, but no one turned up. However, I had a new problem: what to do with the incriminating bottle. I had intended to hide it out there somewhere for later recovery, but I hadn't thought about where. I kept walking and was soon rewarded by an almost entirely fallen-down shed only thirty yards off the road. I made my way to the ruin, careful not to leave prints in the patchy snow, and found a great hidey-hole under a fallen beam.

There was one final step in this ritual dance. Having gone to all this trouble to get a bottle of whiskey, I couldn't go home without at least having a swig. I unscrewed the top and took a small one. I still remember the warmth as it slid down. I was a newcomer to whiskey, but not a virgin, so I didn't cough and splutter. I took another small swallow. Then I waited a bit and had two more. They got bigger and bigger. I probably didn't drink more than two ounces at the most, but it was enough. It warmed my insides. And it did something to my head that came to be a familiar and welcome sensation—but it was new then. It was the "click" that alcoholic Brick speaks of in *Cat on a Hot Tin Roof*. It was a private sensation; it didn't happen the same way in a crowd. When it kicked in, I felt a sort of heightening of my mental faculties. I felt could think more clearly, make plans. All the way home, I daydreamed scenarios for using my newfound treasure—my pint of Four Roses.

From then until graduation, I pretty much always had a bottle of Four Roses hidden somewhere not far from campus. In fact, I didn't drink often or much. Frank and his circle knew about it, but Billy Manley was the only guy in my class with whom I shared my secret. A couple of times, I took him to the hiding place of the moment and we would drink a bit together. But I didn't trust anyone else. I feared news of my stash would be too interesting a tidbit for someone not to want to share.

My little bottle never did become a very big part of my life at SPS. If I had been caught, I would have been thrown right out, which would have changed my life forever. That I risked so much for so little says something about how important drinking had become to me, even then. Having that little bottle marked who I was in my mind. I was someone with a bottle of whiskey on campus.

In time, my visits began to take on a new and more sinister importance. Sometimes, when I felt a bit blue, a little down, alone, I would head out to my friend in the woods for a little one-on-one fellowship. That pull for solitary companionship with alcohol that began at St. Paul's would dog me for many years to come.

My visits to my little hidden bottles became more frequent, and I got cleverer about finding good hiding spots close to, or even on, campus—chinks in walls and holes in trees. When the warm weather brought the foliage, even a good shrub would do. The trick was not to be seen making the same odd detour too often. In my first year, I would go alone or with Billy Manley. Even so, I would change my hiding place regularly. I never wanted to find that someone had beaten me to my stash—no one ever did.

Boys' boarding schools were—surely still are—bastions of secrets handed down from generation to generation. Cooley's little operation was one of these. "The hut" was another. I don't know when it had been built, but it had been lovingly passed on from a group of rule-breakers in one class to kindred spirits in the next. It was the topography that protected it. It was built on a flat piece of land, protected from prying eyes by a steep hill behind it and another steep fall off in front. You had to be right on top of it before you could spot it. Its back half was dug into the hill, and the front consisted of rather well fitted logs, which supported a good tin roof.

Most of us drank and smoked a bit out there, but some just liked being part of the secret. Aside from the forbidden substances, we were pretty good boy scouts. We performed the necessary maintenance and kept our little clubhouse clean and tidy. We brought out bits of this and that to make it more comfortable. A venerable wicker rocking chair was our prized possession, but miscellaneous camp chairs and tables of various sorts made our hideaway pretty homey.

We were good at coming and leaving by different routes so as not to leave a trail. While we did rely on its clever location, we still feared discovery, so we hid any incriminating evidence—cigarettes and liquor—in a metal trunk buried a hundred yards from the hut.

Visits to the hut were not very risky, but my Friday night forays into town were another matter. My first such occurred on a warm Friday night in mid-October of my freshman year, when Frank sought me out on the football field late in the afternoon and told me rather briskly to meet him in the little white pine grove by the main entrance to the school at eleven o'clock. "And oh, bring your bottle and wear black." That's all he told me, but it was all I needed. I was there fifteen minutes early.

We were headed for the town of Concord, four miles away. The drill was to go parallel to the road, but far enough off it so as not to be picked up by headlights of cars going either way. We feared being spotted by masters. We were in good shape, and would pretty much as soon run as walk—and running got you there faster, so we ran much of the way.

Our destination turned out to be a loft in a garage next to a gas station and a little mom-and-pop store on the edge of town. There, a little group of eight or ten Concord High School regulars gathered on Friday nights to smoke and drink a little, play some records, dance a bit, and shoot the breeze. Except for the cigarettes and booze, good clean fun. A few years earlier, a couple of renegade Paulies had tumbled into the gathering and were made right at home. From then on, when from time to time a few preppies showed up, they were welcome. The drill was that we would swing by the store first, pick up some Coke, chips, crackers, and cheese, and then join the party in the loft.

There was an interesting dynamic going. We were the exotics. Guys from the school. It was no secret that it was a rich kids' school. We were rich kids. But what we did was talk about sports, music, girls, parties, cars, camping, and fishing as if we had grown up together. And some of us slow danced. Wasn't dancing cheek-to-cheek with a girl fine? Wasn't that worth all the risk and more?

We used to take the train to school. You could count on seeing six or eight Paulies on Philadelphia's 30th Street platform at the start of any term. Bill Smith, Mort Saunders, and I were the three Philadelphians from my form. A big contingent boarded in New York. The drill was that you had to get off in Boston at either Back Bay or South Station, and cross Boston to North Station to board a new train for Concord, New Hampshire.

The trip that got me into trouble was my return in September for my fourth-form year (tenth grade). I no longer remember whether my actions were premeditated or whether inspiration hit me when I saw a liquor store in the North Station, but by the time I boarded the Concord train, I had a pint of bonded bourbon in my suitcase. And by the time I got to Concord, a good bit of the pint was gone—as was I. What probably saved me from immediate expulsion was the fact that I was still an inexperienced drinker; swigging from that bottle of 100-proof whiskey, showing off, soon put me under, so I passed out pretty early in the ride. By the time I woke up (or was woken up) in Concord, I had slept off the worst of it and, with the help of my friends, made it safely through the school greeting party and into bed. In the morning, I was hungover but not in trouble. Or so I thought.

Boys will talk, however, and word got around that Newlin 2 (Frank was Newlin 1) had gotten plastered on the train from Boston. The problem was that the story reached the faculty, too. When I returned from football practice that afternoon, there was a note on my door: SEE ME, in the big caps used by Mr. Preston, the Simpson housemaster. There was nothing to do but go. Preston was a humorless straight arrow who had gone from St. Paul's to Princeton and back to SPS as a master, without ever stopping in the real world. I figured I knew what he had on his mind, and I was right.

Preston was right out of central casting, trim in his three-piece tweed suit, crew cut hair, and tortoiseshell glasses. His study was more of the same: It was book-lined, sports-trophy-decorated, with leather chairs. He sat me down and came right to the point. He spoke, he said, "more in sorrow than in anger." (He really said that.) It had come to his attention that there had been drinking on the train. I was better than that. That kind of behavior let down the whole team. Think how it reflected on the school to have SPS boys behaving like that on the train. ("Boys," plural. Well, yes, I had passed the bottle around.) His big gun was my parents. Think how disappointed they would be if they found out.

What interested me was what he was revealing that he didn't know. If he had a witness, he would have just nailed me. Most importantly, he never actually accused me of drinking on the train, and he never asked me if I had. It had happened, but who had done it? I figured my best tactic was to just say as little as possible and, above all, admit to nothing. Preston, to my bewilderment, let me get away with it. When he finished his spiel, and it was clearly my turn to speak, I said I certainly didn't want to let anyone down. I was looking forward to a good term—a good year. Then I shut up. We sat there in uncomfortable juxtaposition for a bit—longer for me than for him, I imagine—and then he dismissed me. We shook hands and that was that.

I had other close calls. Once, after a visit to Cooley's, he gave me a couple of cigarettes. I had never taken to smoking and had not even learned to inhale. As I was usually in training for some sport or other, I had a good excuse not to smoke, but sometimes it seemed cool to light up. That afternoon, I had had a bit more of my new bottle before hiding it, and I was feeling pretty mellow as I walked back to the school. I lit up and puffed away happily as I walked. I remember being a bit surprised—startled—to find myself so soon at the south entrance to the school grounds. I insouciantly flipped my butt over the fence onto school property and followed it over, walking jauntily up the main road to my room. I had what would have been a noticeable buzz on and would have almost surely been busted had I met a master, but I encountered no one and was fine by dinnertime.

The climax of my drinking at St. Paul's came two days before graduation. I hadn't planned any escapades. More accurately, I had decided to play it straight. I knew I had been lucky. Now the last term was over and I was home free. I had never been a conscientious student and I didn't have great grades, but I had been told by a master that I had the best English SAT score in my form, and I had had a great Harvard interview. Mirabile dictu, that's where I was headed in the fall. This wasn't the time to screw up.

But it wasn't my call. Not really. Sam Van Dine (his, and some other students' names have been changed to protect the innocent) had been bounced sometime earlier in the year for some infraction or another. The details are fuzzy now and may have been even then. Sam and I had never been particularly close. He was known to have a "bad attitude" and was always suspected by the faculty of breaking rules—especially those prohibiting smoking and drinking. That in itself gave me a reason not to pal around with him too much. His reputation would rub off on me. But now, he was back for graduation, and with a car. He spread the word around to the dozen or so obvious suspects: He had rented a cabin near the lake where parents often stayed over on visiting weekends, and he was giving a party. We weren't to worry about the booze; he would provide everything. We just had to be there. In spite of my good intentions, this was not an invitation the bad boy side of me could refuse.

Many of the details of that evening are gone from my mind. We got there and back in a cab whose driver, like Cooley, had a lock on the illicit SPS trade. He would pick us up and drop us at a dark, prearranged spot near the school. The party itself was what you would expect, maybe not as wild as you might picture. Most of us were as aware as I of how close we were to the finish line, and none of us wanted to get caught. The other cabins were pretty close by and occupied largely by SPS parents. We didn't want to get busted for noise, so we sat around and drank, but mostly not to excess, listened to records, and told tales until late. Sam's car took one bunch back, and the outlaw cab took the others. Everything would have been fine... except for Crandall.

Bobby Crandall (name changed) wasn't really in the drinking set, but he roomed with one of the most serious drinkers in our class, if not the school, so Crandall was just swept along with him. I didn't pay much attention to what either of them were doing or drinking during the evening, but I did notice that sometime around midnight, Crandall had passed out quietly in a corner. At least that's where he was when it came time to go back to school at about two in the morning. I was told later that he had only had a couple of beers but had a light head. Who knows what he drank. In any event, we loaded him into Sam's car, and went back to school. In hindsight, it seems clear that Crandall had more than two beers, was perhaps even dangerously close to alcohol poisoning. But we were oblivious to such risks at the time. To us, it was all part of the adventure, nothing to worry about.

The most dangerous time when you have sneaked out at night is the getting back. My senior year, I lived on the ground floor of Brewster, a fourth-form dormitory where my roommate and I were "supervisors" overseeing the younger students. My preferred route in and out was through my own window, judiciously left open. But that wouldn't help with Crandall. He lived at the end of the hall on the third floor of Upper, the big three-story dorm for seniors. He had to be lugged out of the car, up the outside stairs to the front door, up the stairs to the second floor and then to the third. It's not easy manhandling a completely inert body up two flights of stairs, but four of us each took an extremity and we got him to his room. No matter how badly we didn't want to be caught, there was no way four somewhat in-the-bag seniors were going to be able to carry their drunk friend up the stairs quietly. It was an inherently funny scene, made more so with each bump of his rump on the stair, or each dropped leg. We got the giggles, but no door opened, no curious head poked out, not even a student's.

Getting Crandall into his own room did wake his roommate, Dave Cates, who rather sleepily lent a hand getting Crandall onto his bed. What made Cates's presence noteworthy was that he was school president. But it didn't matter; he was one of us. He had participated in plenty of late evenings himself and had been no stranger to on-campus drinking in our fifth-form year. While he had been pretty clean senior year, he wasn't about to rat out his roommate and his other friends. We said goodbye, wished one another luck and made our way back to our respective beds.

I woke up the next morning, the day before graduation, somewhat worse for wear, but secure in the knowledge that I hadn't been caught, and I hoped—and expected—that the others had fared as well. My first misgivings were at chapel, compulsory for the whole school. Crandall wasn't in his assigned seat. None of the participants in the previous evening's festivities even wanted to be seen talking with one another, but the word on Crandall got around pretty quickly. He hadn't been able to get out of bed in the morning, his housemaster became involved, he was clearly drunk, and it looked as if he was out.

What everyone wanted to know was who had been out with Crandall. Little knots of people gathered all over the campus asking that question. The answer should have been obvious. Sherlock Holmes would have solved the problem easily enough using his "the dog didn't bark" reasoning. Which students were not participating in these fact-finding conversations? Which groups of people who might be expected to know something about after-hours drinking were studiously avoiding contact with one another? Which people known to be friends of Sam Van Dine were avoiding him like the plague?

At the midday meal, my housemaster went out of his way to seek me out, or at least that's how it looked to me. "What's your theory, Bill?"

"Theory?" What could he have on his mind?

"Sure. Crandall certainly wasn't out alone. Who was he partying with?"

"Beats me. Nauman and I were dead to the world." Penny Nauman was my roommate, my best friend, and later my best man. It wouldn't have mattered what Penny had heard happening that night; he "wouldn't have heard anything."

The day passed uneventfully—if my heart banging against my chest as if it were trying to get out was uneventful. As far as I or anyone else could see, there was no systematic hue and cry. There was no investigation. No school authority asked those who might know anything about drinking the previous night to step forward. The last night ceremonies went off as scheduled, and the right people got prizes for the things they did best.

My parents had come up for graduation. They knew a senior had been found drunk and was not going to graduate, but it didn't affect them. Our conversation was about family summer plans. It was 1951, and we were taking our first trip to a Europe still recovering from the war.

When my name was called the next morning, and I went up to shake the rector's hand and get my diploma, I managed to wait until I was back at my chair to unravel and examine it. To my relief, I found it was a real diploma, in Latin, not a blank sheet of paper. The school still did not know who had been with Crandall, and now it never would.

Don't feel too sorry for Bobby Crandall. I don't know what transpired between the Crandall family, SPS, and Yale, but while Crandall didn't walk up to shake the rector's hand on graduation day, he went to Yale in the fall as an SPS graduate, and I don't think he ever had to look back.

It was at St. Paul's that I learned to appreciate secret, solitary drinking. There, too, was where I first felt my need to be a drinker come close to ruining my life.

# 4

## BLACKOUTS

THE SUMMER BEFORE I WENT TO HARVARD WAS marked by a succession of debutante parties—"coming out" parties, where limitless alcohol was available every night. Night after night, some Philadelphia debutante would have her big night, her coming out party, to which large chunks of young Philadelphia society would flock. The grander parties were large dinner dances. Sometimes one girl's parents would give the big dance, and other girls would come out at separate, pre-dance dinners that same night. These could occur at big private houses, clubs, or public places such as hotel ballrooms. Even the most modest were lavish by any normal standards. All liquor, including champagne, flowed freely until one or two in the morning—sometimes until four or five—at which time occasionally a breakfast would be served, and at the June parties, the sun would make an appearance.

Most of the time, my drinking stayed within bounds. But periodically, I would overstep. On one such evening, I experienced my first blackout. The blackout is a well-known phenomenon affecting the serious drinker, including me. Blackouts are unpredictable. Whole days can be lost—more likely are periods of a few hours. The most usual blackout experience is waking up in the morning not knowing what went on the previous night. Sometimes it is the whole evening that is lost. Sometimes only pieces are missing.

The first time this happened to me, I was terrified. I was in my bed at home. It was 9:30 in the morning and the sun poured into the room. From the bed, I could see my dinner jacket hung neatly over a chair in my room and its trousers hanging by the cuffs from the top drawer of my dresser. I waited a beat, got up, and went to the bathroom Frank and I shared in our two-bedroom suite sealed off from the rest of the house by a sliding door. Dress shirt—minus cuff links and studs—white boxers, and socks all lay in the bottom of the laundry hamper. Back in the bedroom, I found the studs and cufflinks, plus the gold pocket watch I always carried in my evening vest, placed neatly in the little porcelain dish I kept for that use only. I appeared to have been functioning perfectly correctly when I got into bed the night before. But I had no recollection at all of the latter part of the evening.

I could remember getting dressed for the party, and I could remember the dinner, or some of it. But I certainly couldn't say how long it lasted. The whole last half of the festivities was a blank. Had I passed out? Had I behaved outrageously? I had no idea. Frank liked to sleep later than I, so I didn't want to wake him. Nor did I wish to make an appearance downstairs. I busied myself by finishing the job of putting my clothes away for their next outing—that very night—and sat down to a book. I couldn't concentrate, but I managed to keep at it. In about an hour I heard Frank stirring so I went in to his room and told him my problem.

He was amused. It happened sometimes, he said— only a few times to him. Sometimes it followed binges when he had really gotten out of hand, but sometimes after nights when from all accounts, he had behaved fine. That, he was happy to report, had been the case the previous night. I had been fine. He had noticed me dancing from time to time throughout the evening and had seen nothing untoward. More to the point, he said, I had been a model of good manners as we made our goodbyes to our debutante hostess and her parents. Nothing to worry about.

Blackouts happpened to me from time to time, but never became a real problem in and of themselves. Some-times, as Frank had said, they followed truly drunken behavior, sometimes not.

## 5

# SLACKING OFF

# AT HARVARD

I TOOK THE TRAINS FROM PHILADELPHIA AND arrived in the early evening. Even now, over sixty-five years later, I can feel the electrifying thrill that physical Harvard, the Yard and the Square, generated in this incoming freshman. Wigglesworth, my upscale freshman dorm, was perfectly located, with one set of windows overlooking the quiet, tree-shaded Harvard Yard and the other the bustle of Massachusetts Avenue and Harvard Square.

I found my room, but no sign of any roommates. I dumped my stuff on a likely bed, unpacking nothing, and hurried downstairs to become part of the scene. The door to my entry opened onto the Yard to a veritable scene from a Currier and Ives print—an elaborate network of footpaths criss-crossing between stone or brick buildings and tall trees, redolent of New England in the fall. It was all too calm for my mood; Harvard Square and its commercial buzz held the greater draw. I button-hooked around to the left and found myself standing on Massachusetts Avenue in the bright lights of Harvard Square.

I teach writing these days, and I introduce the difference between subjective and objective description. Objectively, Harvard Square was quite ordinary. Massachusetts Avenue, Brattle Street, and Harvard Streets came together to form an undistinguished island occupied by a large, international newsstand and the entrance to the subway. Cars whizzed by. Much of the commercial activity was entirely ordinary—a little commuter bar on the corner, some chain eateries, a movie house. True, some establishments catered to the college trade. The Harvard Coop sold books and Harvard paraphernalia along with nearly everything else. There was Schoenhof's for interesting used books, Leavitt and Pierce for pipes and esoteric tobacco, and J. Press for preppy clothes. But there was nothing special on the objective level.

For an incoming freshman, however, stepping into that heady mix for the first time, objectivity didn't exist. Something mysterious occurred. An exhilaration came not from any of the external stimuli, but from some collection of expectations which had been building for years. This was not just any street corner; this was Harvard Square. I was, and would be for the next four years, a part of it, part of Harvard College. The lights, sounds, and smells took on a singular, thrilling life of their own.

That night, I walked for an hour just exploring the area bordering on the Square. Most of the shops were closed. Still, the excitement in the air was palpable. The people on the streets were just people, but because this was Harvard, I knew for a fact that their secret stories could never be mundane, only fascinating. I was now a part of it all, and a part of their stories. I walked down toward the river and the dormitories, called "houses," for upperclassmen. The older students were, for the most part, not back in town yet. The handsome, distinctive brick buildings held the promise of mystery and intrigue. I walked back up Holyoke Street and back into the lights and bustle of the Square. Then the side streets, Dunster, Plympton, and Mount Auburn.

When I had exhausted the commercial area, I headed back into the Yard, crisscrossing it, crossing paths with other pedestrians, some seemingly just strolling, others with important (never mundane) destinations. Back into the lights of the Square. It was late when I finally pulled myself away from that heady atmosphere and went to bed.

What I find especially interesting, as I recall that first night in Cambridge, is that I have no memory of having had anything to drink. I, who had spent much of my time and energy at my cooped-up boarding school procuring alcohol and arranging for places and ways to drink it, found myself alone in Harvard Square for the first time, plenty of places to stop and have a drink, and for all I remember of the evening, I didn't have so much as a sip. The whole experience was clearly so intoxicating that it needed no enhancement.

I did not remain so abstemious through my freshman year, let alone for all four years at Harvard. Paulies are known to go off the deep end their first year of college, not studying as they should, but rather coasting on their good preparation and abusing the freedom they were denied at St. Paul's by various overindulgences, especially of alcohol. I fit both parts of that mold. Early on, I developed a mind-set that, to my shame and sorrow, stayed with me to some extent throughout my entire college career. I thought it better to get an OK grade without having studied than to study hard, get a better grade, and learn a lot in the bargain. This attitude surely stemmed in part from early experiences as a freshman, where it became clear that my good private school preparation stood its possessors in such good stead that it was easy to coast.

I adhered to this philosophy at the expense not only of my education, but of my pleasure. For example, all freshmen had to take the basic writing course, General Education AHF. I have no idea now, and may not have known then, what the initials stood for. It met three times a week, and written work was assigned at every meeting of the class. Gen Ed was largely, if not exclusively, taught by graduate students. The assignments were, at least in the beginning, brief exercises to familiarize the students with various writing techniques. I remember one assignment requiring us to take a piece of writing which was slanted in one direction, and slant it the other way by subtly changing some adjectives and the emphasis. I had a good time turning an ad for an automobile around by making speed, horsepower, and sleek styling sound like undesirable characteristics. I was too much praised for my efforts by my young section man, who gave me an A for that and for everything else I turned in. About halfway into the course, he apologized for making someone of my talents limit myself to these simple drills. There was my opening. I agreed with him. I said that I would much prefer to do something "substantive." Instead of the daily papers, couldn't I write a longer paper that would really let me get my teeth into something? He hadn't wanted to go that far, but I persuaded him, so I was excused from doing the three weekly exercises that I had so enjoyed, and which were so clearly useful to me. Instead, I was turned loose on some amorphous longer, more "interesting" project.

The result was a disaster. I put off doing the longer paper until the last moment and then turned in a poorly written piece of derivative fiction—short stories had never been my forte. He gave me the poor grade that my effort deserved and a mediocre grade for the term; and I lost the chance to learn something about writing.

I recount this story because it is illustrative of my attitude toward my work. When I did it, I enjoyed it. I loved reading Plato and Aristotle, and I loved John Finley's lectures about the *Iliad* and the *Odyssey,* but I couldn't let myself be seen taking them too seriously.

The perception others had of me influenced my attitude toward drink, too. Just as I did not want to be seen to study too hard, I wanted to be thought of as someone who held his liquor well, knew about alcohol and wine, and used them often and copiously. Having drunk a lot was good, but losing control was bad. The problem was, even then, that I found it hard to always stay on the right side of the line. Parties were a problem. It was easy to have just a bit too much.

Then, in the spring term of my sophomore year, the unthinkable happened, unrelated to college or my drinking. It was early Saturday afternoon. I had come back to my room in Wigglesworth for something or other, and was just leaving when the telephone rang. I was in a hurry and almost didn't answer it, but I wasn't quite blasé enough to walk out on a ringing phone. It was Mother.

"Billy, I have some very bad news." I'm not sure if I said anything or if she just went on. I think I just waited.

"It's about Frankie." Another pause. "He's been in an automobile accident." She sounded unreal. She wasn't crying, but she didn't sound like herself. I felt a terrible coldness. I think I knew then.

Mother again: "He has been badly hurt."

This time I did speak. "Is he going to get better?"

Mother didn't speak for what seemed like an eternity. I could hear her sobbing, and I knew for sure. She finally got it out. "No, Billy, he's dead." More sobbing. I have no recollection of the conversation beyond that. I don't know what I said to try to comfort her or what I said about arrangements. I don't remember saying goodbye and hanging up. Of course I would go right home.

My mind turned away from my brother, my dead brother, to the details of the moment. I had to pack. What would I bring? I had no idea how long I would be staying. I went about mechanically gathering the necessaries: Clean white shirts. Did I have a black four-in-hand? Only a knit one. Was my grey suit pressed? Passably. While I packed, my mind would flash back to Frank. I had been down to the University of Virginia campus to see him just the month before. It was my first time there, and I had loved everything about it.

My mind kept filling with images of Frank with his roommates. He had lived on the edge of the campus in a picture-perfect little brick house. One of the roommates,

Ned, his last name now lost to time, was a notorious comic. I couldn't believe their house could be like that all the time. Laughter everywhere, at everything. People coming by. A constant party. Never in my four years at Harvard did I see anything like the hilarity of that little band of merrymakers in that house. It would wane, fade, but then catch its breath, and they were off again, Ned masterminding the mirth.

People would come by in waves, but we went places, too, to other houses. I always rode with Frank in his little red MG convertible—top down. Cambridge was still raw in March, but Charlottesville was balmy; May saw it in full spring bloom. We were always welcome at the next party. Where had we been? The merriment could now begin! Certainly there was tons of drink available, but no one was out of control. No one was doing anything outrageous. Drink didn't drive us. The party did.

My recurring images of those hours were all of Frank. Frank and his wife Joan answering the door, welcoming people in. Frank pouring drinks. Frank flirting with the girls—there were always girls, pretty girls, Joan the prettiest. But the most haunting image, the one that kept coming back, was Frank at the wheel of his little red MG, looking for all the world like an ad for a hair product or a tooth whitener, looking like a young god, laughing, with the wind in his hair. I don't know when the reality of his death hit me, but not then, not as I was packing. He couldn't be dead.

Dad had hated that car, and Frank knew it when he bought it. Dad's brother had been killed in a convertible and Dad wanted nothing to do with them. But Frank would have it, and he bought it. I have never fully understood why he did that.

The details of the accident were recounted to me many times but they are not clear in my mind. I think I never wanted them to be. Frank was not driving, He was asleep in the passenger seat. Passed out from drinking? It's likely. But it was not emphasized. A friend and he were driving home, the friend at the wheel. It was slippery and the car skidded and turned over. Both Frank and the driver seemed miraculously unhurt. They were taken to a hospital, examined and released, but as Frank was leaving he fainted. More tests. His liver was crushed. Nothing to do.

I had a mission. I had to get my necessaries together, funeral things, and I had to get home. My parents would need help. Mother would need help. Frank was the golden boy. They would not be able to handle the loss. I hadn't even talked to Dad. I hadn't even talked to my sister. I had to get to Philadelphia, to the town of Wayne and to our home, Sunny High.

I didn't have enough money, just a twenty and change. There were no credit cards in 1952, no ATMs. You had to lay in money for weekends. I had been provident enough for normal circumstances. I hadn't had expensive plans for the weekend and the cash I had would have seen me through, but now I needed more. I needed the Harvard Provision Company—the Pro. That was the principal Harvard liquor store, and on weekends one of its accepted functions for regular customers—among whom I numbered—was to cash checks. They did a brisk business, but twenty was the standard outside limit. I needed more.

I closed my suitcase, saw no one I knew, left no note, just crossed Massachusetts Avenue at the light and walked over to Mount Auburn Street and the Pro. I usually dealt with red-haired Fred. He knew I lived in Wigglesworth, knew I liked bonded, 100-proof bourbon, preferably Old Forester. Fred was cordial enough, that was his business, but he couldn't give me more than twenty. I would have to see the boss. I knew who the boss was, but we had never gone beyond welcoming nods. Now I needed his help. I was shameless. I pulled a long face and quietly told him, eyes downcast, that I had just learned my brother had died in an automobile accident at the University of Virginia and I needed cash to fly to Philadelphia. Could he cash me a check for fifty? "Sure," he said, "I'm sorry for your loss." I wrote the check, he gave me the money and I took the subway to Logan airport.

I was ashamed. It had been over an hour since I had learned of Frank's death, and I hadn't shed a tear. Worse, when softening up the guy with his hand on the purse, I had actually faked grief. Now I began to cry. The car was nearly empty and no one paid much attention to me. When I got to the station, I sat on the bench on the platform and missed a couple of shuttle buses to the terminal while I sobbed some tears out of my system.

Home was as full of tears as Charlottesville had been of laughter. At any one time, any of us could be fine, but then something would set one of us off again, and as likely as not, all four of us, Mom, Dad, Lucy Bell, and I, would be sobbing together. Mother never failed to put the best face on everything. That's who she was. But she was defeated by Frank's death. It had no good face. She went through the motions, but couldn't get beyond them. When the doorbell rang, Mother didn't go to answer it. She still knew how to be polite. She could welcome newcomers when they made their way to her. But the life was out of her.

Dad always had a way, when he wanted, of retiring into himself even in company. That's what he did. Physically, he mostly stayed in his usual chair in the room where Frank's body lay. He would get up when others entered. He would say hello. But then he would sit down again, and retreat.

Arrangements had to be made. Ministers came and gave comfort, but they also received instructions. What hymns, what lessons, who would read, who would sit where. These details had to be settled. The service would be followed by what would amount to a big cocktail party at Sunny High, and that had to be arranged. Mother must have been functioning better than I remember, because many of these details almost surely fell to her.

The service itself is a blur. What I particularly remember is how large the UVA group was, and how glad I was that it was they and I who made up the pallbearers, not the professionals in their black suits. It's the Charlottesville contingent I remember most at the post-service reception. Sunny High was a great party house. It had a drive that came in from one street and led out onto another, with most of its parking up by the former stable. I had parked up there, away from the house, leaving room for old folks in the close-in spots. On the way back to the house, I came up behind two guys I didn't know, hugging one another. I heard one say as I went by, "He was a prince."

He was a prince. Prince Hal, perhaps, but a prince. I have said he was the golden boy, but he was trouble, too. He had drunk too much from early adolescence, and while he could, and often did, get fabulous grades, sometimes he didn't. He would do things like show up for an interview with the naval ROTC without having shaved. He and Joan Jackson, his then-girlfriend, had eloped, and had set up house on the edge of the campus. Joan told us she was pregnant, and that Frank had known it. I have always wanted to believe that. As with his buying the convertible in the face of Dad's strong opposition, I always wondered why he wanted to elope with Joan. She would have been so warmly welcomed into the family. Now we would never know how all this talent would have played out. Would the drink have dragged him down? Would he have quit and soared? Something in between?

The last guests went home, and after a couple of days, it was time for me to go back to Cambridge. There were still plenty of tears at Sunny High. I came up behind Mother shortly before leaving. She was sobbing, and I put my hands on her shoulders to comfort her. "I'll be all right," she said. "I was just thinking about heaven, and I worried that Frankie wouldn't like it there. But then I thought of all the interesting people in heaven and I realized it would be all right."

I hoped she was right.

Just how Frank's death affected me, I will never know. My drinking was already off to a good start on the road to abuse. If he had lived, I imagine, I would have drunk too much in order to keep him company. Now that he was gone, did I have to drink to keep a part of him alive?

## 6

# HARVARD,
# POST-FRANK

NOTWITHSTANDING THE GRIEF I FELT, SCHOOL wouldn't wait for me, so I had to get right back. Life went on. At Harvard, there was no question in my mind that I wanted to join one of the eight "final clubs." That's what most of my friends would do. The clubs were terrible anachronisms. They only accommodated about ten percent of the class, mostly WASPs from private schools. I was a liberal Democrat even then (in spite of my staunch Republican parents), but I wasn't strong enough in my convictions to refuse the privileges my birth and upbringing accorded me.

The clubs had cool clubhouses in the center of campus. They were not residential, but members could hang out, take lunch on weekdays and enjoy periodic dinners and other special events. The clubs were then for men only, and allowed women inside the premises only on special occasions. (The Spee Club, the one I joined, has since opened its doors to women members.)

In the fall of our sophomore year, our class was "punched." The clubs would invite sophomores who interested them to little cocktail parties called punches. As the "punching season" progressed, small dinners were added, along with Sunday lunches at the comfortable houses of interested club alumni. Finally, on an appointed day, all the clubs sent emissaries with written invitations around to the dorm rooms of the chosen. As I remember it, you were to respond by the end of the day. By the time the elections came around, I was still being punched by two clubs I would have been pleased to join—plus two others. My selection was simplified when only one of my preferred clubs elected me. So I joined the Spee Club.

The Spee Club had a great brick building with a walled garden at 76 Mount Auburn Street, right around the corner from the main entrance to my house—Lowell. The Spee was certainly a bastion for the privileged, but it had a more liberal record than most. It had been the first to accept Catholic members (that's how JFK and Bobby got in), the first to accept a Jew, the first to accept a black member, the first to have a black president, and finally, the first to accept women. But in my time, it was all male and still pretty WASPy. We clubbies tended to dress alike in our tweed suits, or gray flannels and tweed jackets, and nice ties. But for all the civilized veneer, drinking was an important part of what went on.

The second-floor bar at the Spee was a beautifully paneled room with nicely carved wood doors leading to every member's own liquor locker, and there was beer on tap. Before the daily lunches, it was a lively place. Not everyone took all their lunches at the club—for one thing, meals at the houses were already paid for as part of room and board. But even if they weren't going to stay for lunch, many members came by for a drink or just for the conviviality. Evenings were similar. The Spee was busy at the traditional cocktail time and there was a weekly dinner.

I used the Spee a lot. It fit into the role I had written for myself—or had fallen into. It was a good place for someone who wasn't going to grind away, the gentleman bon vivant. Drinking was a part of that life, but not the defining part.

The Spee became an important part of my life. I spent much of the time when I had nothing else to do—classes or study—there. I would read *The New York Times* in the morning room before my first class, stop in between classes, often have lunch there, and check in before dinner and again before going to bed. Its location on the route back to my house was certainly a major reason I stopped in so often.

Another reason to be at the club was the conviviality. At most times, there was apt to be someone there to interact with. I have a somewhat split personality. Part of me seeks, enjoys, and even needs contact with others, but I also have a solitary, even secretive side. Mr. Congenial was fed by the Spee Club, but the secret me had his place in my life, too, and its space began to enlarge around this time.

I have never seen a psychiatrist in any serious way. I did go to one about my drinking briefly, but it wasn't someone I could relate to and I don't think it helped me understand myself any better. Maybe a shrink could have told me how important alcohol was to the development of my solitary side at this time in my life. My suspicion is that it played a big role. I have said that I wanted to be known as someone who drank a good bit, but drinking could never be seen to be an end in itself. I drank, I wanted the world to see, because I was living large, and drinking was a part of that. But I did not want the world to see the whole picture.

So sometimes I would go out on my own, just to sit alone in some anonymous bar and drink. I had a variety of haunts for a wide range of moods. One favorite was right on Massachusetts Avenue, smack in the middle of Harvard Square. Hard to believe, but in all my years in Cambridge, I never once saw anyone there I could identify as a Harvard student. It was a local hangout, a place where, if you sat near the window, you could see the buses coming; you could sip your whiskey or your beer until your bus heaved into view and then finish your drink in a couple of swallows and run out to catch it.

I was a dimey drinker there. A dimey was a draft beer, which in those enlightened days sold for a dime. A dollar in your pocket was ten draft beers—a night on the town. I was a daydreamer there, sitting alone, listening to the jukebox playing that great fifties music—Johnnie Ray ("Cry"), Patti Page ("Tennessee Waltz"), Nat King Cole, Pat Boone ("Love Letters in the Sand"), Teresa Brewer ("Till I Waltz Again with You"), Tony Bennett, Perry Como—and the show tunes—*Guys and Dolls, The King and I, Gigi.* They belong to that bar, that time—but they only began to get really good when my dimes were about half gone.

Other times I would take the subway across the Charles River into Boston. I had found several nice quiet spots, some in hotels, all with some kind of music, all where I could be anonymous. Sometimes I would chat someone up at the bar, but more likely not. By now, my drinking was increasingly daily and solitary, and predictably, my school work was suffering.

Apart from the Spee Club, there were other social hubs and watering hole opportunities at which to drink socially, all of which fed my gregarious side. At the Spee, you could often get up a gang to go somewhere else. There was always something going on at the Hasty Pudding, another members-only eating and drinking establishment. Most members of final clubs belonged to the Pudding, and many non-clubmen did besides. You knew everyone at your final club; not so at the Pudding.

And there was always Cronin's, Harvard's most popular drinking spot. At the time, Harvard owned that building right in the heart of Harvard Square, and some time between my graduation from college and my return to Cambridge for graduate school, the university had kicked Cronin's out and turned the premises into an administrative building. My grown-up daughter, who is of a generation more attuned to the dangers of college drinking, says this makes perfect sense to her. But I think Cronin's was a great community builder, and that closing it was a mistake. A college needs its Cronin's, a big noisy joint with lots of booths overflowing with students; with waitresses making their way through the crowd with platters of hamburgers and big pitchers of beer. "I'll meet you at Cronin's." What do kids do now? We would go over to Cronin's and join the crowd, calling across to friends at other tables, generally adding to the confusion and merriment.

I have never been very good at keeping personal history in my head, and which year I did what. My impression of those years is that my sophomore year was a bad one, not much study and too much drinking, but that I began to straighten up in my junior year. As senior year came along,

I began to smarten up even more. For one thing, Louisa had entered my life in a big way, and we were engaged to be married right after my graduation. We were young—on our wedding day in 1955, she was 19 and I was 22. I wasn't that eager to get married early, but I knew if I were to marry Louisa, I had to act fast. Otherwise, someone would beat me to her. She was beautiful, talented, generous, and had an infectious laugh, still one of the things I love most about her.

She already knew me pretty well, knew I didn't study as much as I should, and knew I drank too much. She, on the other hand, had thrown herself into her courses and thrived on Harvard's academic side. Up to a point, she reluctantly tolerated my somewhat rakish side. That I was the antithesis of her father, a bank president (whom she adored and respected), could work to my benefit. She was prepared to give me the benefit of the doubt—to see the real me, the good me, the one my mother could see, the one who was going through a youthful phase but who would come out all right in the end. To keep Louisa happy, I didn't have to become a complete square, but I had to go to class most of the time and I couldn't get drunk—at least not at inopportune times.

I knew if I didn't keep my part of the unspoken bargain, and behave like someone she could marry and be happy with, Louisa wouldn't stay with me, so I did my best. I cut back on time at the Spee, and stepped up the studying—general exams were ahead, and to fail them meant not graduating. There is no way Louisa would have married me if I had not graduated with my class in June of 1955. Senior year, I even had time to be in the Hasty Pudding's annual show, the one in which all the girl parts are played by guys. (I had a guy role.) Some friends of mine had written the Hasty Pudding show for our year, and they insisted they had written a part just for me. They were not impressed by my protestations that I couldn't sing. Neither could Rex Harrison they said, and look what he did in *My Fair Lady*. What's a guy to do? I took the part. So senior year ended on a high note. I passed my general exams and graduated in good standing with my class. I didn't attend graduation; Louisa and I were married on the very day, which annoyed my father.

The college years were over. They had changed my drinking habits. I drank every day now, and often too much. Perhaps "often too much, but sometimes I got drunk" would be a more accurate way to put it. Moreover, I had further developed the habit of secret, solitary drinking. It was at Harvard that I began to learn the skill of being a high-functioning alcoholic. I couldn't stay sober, but I could appear sober to the outside world. In those early days I could even fool Louisa some of the time—or I thought I could.

I was still a functioning person, but I fear that by the time Louisa and I left Cambridge to start a new life, the die may have already been cast.

# 7

## EARLY WARNINGS: HONEYMOON, ARMY, AND GRADUATE SCHOOL

WE BEGAN A WHOLE NEW PHASE OF OUR LIVES. I have been writing about the drinking habits of a kid and then a student. Suddenly, we were a married couple. What mattered now was how my drinking would affect this new entity—our family.

It became an issue between us early in our courtship. Louisa always knew I was a bit wild. I was one of the bad Newlin boys who drove too fast, drank a bit much, and had an eye for the girls. If that's not how I was perceived, it was not for lack of trying. Did I feel I had to maintain that reputation of wildness for Frank? Maybe.

That said, I wasn't nearly the rogue I wanted to make myself out to be, which was all to the good because Louisa would not have wanted someone who overstepped by very far the narrow bounds set by our group of peers on the Main Line. On the drinking front, high alcohol consumption was all right for a boy, and the ability to "hold one's liquor" won points. An accompanying excess of exuberance was acceptable and even at times appreciated, but any loss of control was frowned on. The obvious side effects of being drunk—slurred speech or an unsteady gait—were beyond the pale. You could have all the champagne you wanted so long as you still cut a dashing figure on the dance floor, made sense when you talked, and could be relied on to drive your girl home safely.

These were subjective judgments, and there was the obvious disconnect between my definition of how much drinking was too much and Louisa's. In those early years, however, while I was a pretty heavy drinker, for the most part I was able to stay within the prescribed bounds.

From the very beginning, however, my drinking was a threat to our relationship. She was the little woman, putting a brake on her man's tendency to drink more than she wanted. I was the guy, always pushing for another drink to keep the party going. Neither of us had any inkling what a dangerous cliff we were skirting—how dangerous alcohol was and how important it was not to let it get the upper hand.

An early warning sign should have been at an engagement party given for us by an aunt of Louisa's in Princeton. I slipped just close enough to the wrong side of the line that Louisa insisted on being the one to drive us back to Philadelphia. It was a good call. The fact that I couldn't be relied on to show myself in the best light when I was being introduced to Louisa's extended family should have been a major signal that there was trouble ahead. Our youth was part of the problem. Louisa was eighteen. Too young to understand the pitfalls of her role as the enabler. She did not even know what an enabler was. By driving me home, she shielded me from the effects of my overindulgence, which allowed me to think I had gotten away with it.

We were married at a large, formal wedding, and I am happy to report I comported myself admirably. After a couple of days of rest in New York, our plan was to have a honeymoon, starting in Spain with a week at the classy Hotel Formentera on the island of Majorca. A major memory from that experience was the angelic, adolescent girl flamenco singer (flamenco was new to us) whose voice is etched forever in our shared memory. We decided she expressed in song the passion we were experiencing much better than we could in words. We then bought two motorized, pedal assisted bicycles, and spent six weeks or so biking around Spain. As an aside, I will admit, of course, this extended honeymoon was an indefensible indulgence, but

I have never regretted it for a moment—not as we were doing it and never in the sixty-three years since.

The week at the Formentera had been first class all the way, but from then on our plan was to stay in simple—but charming—accommodations. Remember, we were rich. This was 1955, the dollar was king and all Americans in Europe were rich. Our bible was Fodor's *Europe on Five Dollars a Day*. (For example, our room and board—three meals a day including wine, with laundry thrown in—on the island of Formentera, the smallest inhabited Balearic, cost 75 cents a day a person. I admit there was no running water, and this was an exception, but still....) The Balearics were a treat, but we had to move on. We toured some of mainland Spain, putting the bikes on trains for the long hauls. To close out the Spanish stretch of our honeymoon, we biked across the Pyrenees to Pau in France (often pedaling to assist our little machines). From there we went to Italy by train, where we joined Louisa's traveling family and my sister. We were a somewhat incongruous group. There was the square, parental generation—my mother- and father-in-law—Mr. Foulke (whom I called Uncle Bill) in his ubiquitous tie, and Mrs. Foulke (Aunt Louisa) in her predictable classic suit. Next came the newlyweds, Louisa and me in our Spanish espadrilles. Then the college kids— my younger sister, Lucy Bell, and Louisa's younger brother, Walter. We were a jumble of Newlins and Foulkes—sisters, brothers, married couples—and the hotel clerks were thoroughly muddled. At summer's end, everyone else went home—as Americans do at the end of summer. But not Louisa and me. We stayed on.

Our extended honeymoon was the fruit of the first of several times in our married life that I have made a quite obviously self-indulgent choice. We had been at war with Korea when I entered Harvard and, with many of my friends, I had joined an ROTC program to guarantee we wouldn't be drafted out of college before graduation. The downside was that ROTC brought with it a two-year active duty commitment. My self-indulgent act was thinking ahead about how lovely it would be to begin our marriage with a prolonged European stay. When the Army asked when I wanted to begin my service, I casually answered February. The army was accommodating and that became the date I told everyone we had to begin our service. Our families all wanted us to come home at the end of the summer and do something responsible, like get a job, until the Army needed us, but we were far away and in command of our destinies.

Fall was approaching. The season had always meant going back to school, so that's what we did. We headed to Paris first, where we enrolled in courses at the Alliance Française. We loved our Paris time, and Paris marked us as its own forever. It has become our second home. We stayed in the Hotel Perryève on the rue Madame. The longer we stayed, the better room we got, until we had one which, by leaning out the window, gave us a view of the Jardin du Luxembourg.

We loved Paris itself, but were not meeting many French students and English was the lingua franca of the foreigners, so we decided to leave Paris and enroll in the Cours pour les Etrangers at the University of Grenoble. That was a good decision. We took classes with other foreign students and we had lots of contact with the French students with whom we nearly always spoke French. French was the dominant language of our social life. We had good fun, and we skied a lot, but it was not time wasted. We also learned much more French, which stood us in good stead once I entered the Foreign Service and received a posting to Paris. Louisa and I still have good friends from those months.

Booze remained a problem, but at this stage, not a defining one. That's not what we brought away from those months. While I still had a tendency to want to drink more than Louisa wanted me to, our differences were in the context of the wife trying to reform her man. Here, as in other places, Louisa largely concurs with my take on how she saw things then. She acknowledges that she was an enabler before she even knew what the word meant. As she puts it, she saw what she wanted to see.

When we got to Paris, I couldn't wait to sit in one of the cafés, so temptingly described by Hemingway, where they kept track of your drinks by stacking your saucers. I thought it was a clear sign of great sophistication to sit behind a significant stack of little plates. At meals, certainly at dinner, I thought it was a sign of weakness to order anything less than a bottle of wine. A demi-carafe would have suited Louisa fine.

At Grenoble, my drinking situation was very different from the Harvard years. At Harvard I had much time to myself. Drinking alone was one of the ways my drinking became established. At Grenoble, Louisa and I were almost always together. Drinking alone was never an option. Still, I wanted to drink more than most of our fellow students; I would be the one who suggested a second bottle of red wine "to go with the cheese," who wanted wine instead of coffee at a midmorning café break, and who brought an extra bottle of wine to a party ostensibly as a "house present" but as much because I didn't want to feel guilty for finishing a bottle before the night was over. But I don't want to believe that an outside observer would have called me a drunk, and I don't think Louisa yet saw alcohol as a major problem. I was aware I was drinking more than Louisa realized and that alcohol was important to me, but I, too, thought my relationship with alcohol was something we—I—could handle.

We had milked our extended honeymoon for as long as we could. The Army needed me, and this time we obeyed docilely. We came home, spent a few weeks catching up with the family, and then drove to Fort Bliss, Texas, for a couple of months of an officer's orientation course. It was there I was to get my all-important ongoing two-year assignments. I was given a form on which we were to list our preferences. In order, I enthusiastically and naively listed the postings I most hoped to receive:

1) French-speaking Europe
2) any Europe, or
3) any overseas.

Dreamer. What I got was Georgia.

Happily, some under-the-table trading was possible. I learned about a southern guy who was really upset because he was assigned to Hawaii, where he had been told that half the population was non-white. An assignment to Georgia was going home for him, so we managed to arrange the trade. That's how Louisa and I got assigned to two years at Schofield Barracks in Hawaii. We drove the rest of the way across the country, spent a few days in San Francisco— which enchanted us both and to which we swore we would return to live when the Army was finished with me—and then flew to Hawaii. This was in 1956—only 15 years after the bombing of Pearl Harbor.

At first, we were billeted in a luxury hotel right on the beach at Waikiki. The whole situation was right out of a travel brochure. I would go off to "work" at Schofield Barracks and Louisa would look for a place to live. For a day or two, she counted herself lucky to be living in luxury on Waikiki Beach. But Louisa's not a beach-sitter, so before long we were out of there. We were out strolling around one evening, on the lookout as always for an interesting place to live, when we spotted a four-story building with what looked like tropical gardens, with small trees and large ferns growing at the corners of the roof itself. There could be no doubt, those were little penthouse apartments. We looked at each other with the same thought: It couldn't hurt to ask. It wasn't even hard to find the super, who greeted us with the quite remarkable news: One of those apartments was coming up for rent in a couple of weeks and, because they were fourth-floor walk-ups, they were even affordable. We signed on the dotted line.

In one sense, however, Louisa was no better off than she had been before she found the apartment. She still had nothing to do. Serendipity struck again. She—not yet graduated from college—applied for and got a job teaching virtually all subjects to a class of sixth graders at Epiphany Day School, a small private school with largely Asian students. Louisa had never so much as taught a single class before, and she found the first few days so difficult that she tried to quit. Father Linscott, the head of school, just laughed at her. He couldn't let her quit. How on earth could he replace her at the beginning of the school year at any price, let alone for $125 a month? So she stuck it out and had an experience that may have been life-defining. Teaching in secondary school became her life's work.

As for me, this was the first time I had a real job with a routine. I found some other young officers living in Waikiki, and working at Schofield Barracks, so we carpooled over the mountain to our base. Our routine on the way home was to stop at the gas station at the pass to get some beer to ease the trip down the mountain. Most guys got one can. I always got two. I got a little flak for that, but mostly from a real penny-pincher who thought it was just a waste of money. Louisa knew we had beer on the way home, but none of the guys ever betrayed me by revealing who the big guzzler was.

I kept the drinking under pretty good control. I don't know how I would have managed to find a way to drink on duty and, except for the beer on the way home, there was no temptation. For the rest of the time, Louisa and I were together. That doesn't mean I didn't always try to sneak a little more drinking in than everybody else in a situation. Nor does it mean I didn't get drunk from time to time. One notable slip was at a promotion party. The person promoted was not from our battalion, so Louisa didn't feel close enough to the guy to attend. I went alone and took advantage of my freedom to overindulge, after which I passed out in my car.

When I didn't come home, Louisa got scared and called an officer in our battalion she trusted, and explained the situation. He guessed right, went and found our car, and me passed out, near the party. He woke me up and accompanied me home. Humiliation. Mostly for Louisa, embarrassed to be married to such a jerk. My savior made light of it. Getting drunk at promotion parties was part of army tradition, he kindly said. Still, incidents like that made it impossible for Louisa to count on me to stay sober, and were damaging to our relationship. But I didn't think either of us took my unreliability as a dangerous sign of trouble ahead. Louisa, however, has said that she saw this incident as a danger sign.

Our first son, Bill, was born during that time, but his arrival didn't make a sober man of me. I perceived no real problem and therefore had no incentive to reform.

The Army was followed by the Harvard Business School (HBS). We moved to Cambridge, Massachusetts, where we shared a little house in North Cambridge with another couple—we had the front; they had the back. He and I shared a fondness for whiskey. I was happy enough with bourbon, but he affected a weakness for Irish whiskey. Irish was costly, however, so bourbon was what we mostly drank. He liked a drink well enough, but it was clear early on that he could take it or leave it. I was no longer in that camp. I had begun to count on my evening drink, and I was unhappy if I didn't get it. Up to this point, although I regularly drank more than most of the people I was with and got noticeably drunk from time to time, my drinking at home was overt, out in the open. I think it was then, in our little house at 59 Rice Street, that I hid my first bottle, so I could sneak a drink when I wanted. I found a good spot in the basement, and it wasn't hard to make up reasons to go down there if I felt the urge. Just one pull from the bottle would make a new man out of me.

It was also at Rice Street that I first began to sneak drinks from the liquor closet. Stocking the liquor closet was my domain. I wasn't always the most reliable person about thinking ahead and keeping the household well stocked with necessities. It was not unheard of for us to be short on rock salt when hit by a snow storm. I could, however, be relied on to keep the liquor cabinet well supplied. When I was busy fixing drinks, or putting bottles away after a party, it was easy to have a swig or two. Who could be the wiser?

I once happened to be looking into someone's liquor closet with one of my brothers-in-law. We could see that nearly every bottle had been drained so that only about a quarter of the bottle was left. I didn't think anything of it, but he remarked, "There's the closet of an alcoholic." His explanation for the nearly uniformly depleted bottles was that someone was using that closet for his regular fix, and he took it from the fullest bottle, so no bottle would be emptied (and need replenishing) soon. I am not sure this was a good plan, because it ensured that when it did become necessary to replenish, a major load of obscure bottles would need to be carted into the house. I did have to recognize that I was not alone in my little deception. I was doing just what that guy did. If Louisa ever wondered why we went through so much Cointreau, Benedictine, and the more obscure liqueurs, she never let on.

Business school was hard, and there was a lot of pressure. The nemesis of most first-year HBS students was the Written Analysis of a Case (WAC). These were due Fridays before midnight. There was a slot in a door through which students slipped their papers. On the tick of midnight, you could hear some sadistic graduate student on the other side of the door slide the box away from its spot under the slot. Any paper dropped through the slot from then on would drop to the floor—with an automatic markdown in one's grade. Once I had my Friday WAC salted away, it was a big temptation to turn to alcohol to relax. This may be where another of my unhealthy habits took root. A good time to drink too much—to get a little drunk—was just before bed. That had the obvious advantage that once you were safely tucked into bed, no one could tell how drunk you were. After a hard WAC, or on any stressful night, I was apt to use either my hidden bottle or something from the liquor closet to tuck away a couple—or a few—big swigs. Then to bed. It may be hard for the non-alcoholic to see that just lying in bed with a buzz would be desirable, but for someone under the thrall of that drug, it had its perverse pleasure.

I have said that the WACs generated a lot of pressure. That resulted in a repeated behavior perhaps worth recording here. Several times, perhaps as often as three or four, when I was feeling especially pressured, and Louisa was in bed asleep and I was glued to whatever project had me buffaloed, I would get out the lovely little English, Westley Richards 12-gauge shotgun my father had given to me, put it together, load it, and just sit with it crooked over one arm and a bottle of bourbon in my hand. I would nurse the bottle for half an hour or so, being careful to take only tiny sips, for I still had a paper to finish. Then I would put the gun and the bottle away, go back to my desk, finish my assignment, and go to bed. I don't think I was ever in danger of doing myself harm, and at no other time of my life did I do anything like this.

Perhaps the thing the Harvard Business School was best known for then was its vaunted "case method" of teaching. The way that worked was that assignments were little stories outlining problems in a particular discipline. Marketing, accounting, production, etc. The cases were simple at first and became increasingly complex. For the first year, the whole class was broken into sections of about one hundred students each. These sections met for every session of every subject for the whole first year. The professors were very non-directive, so the students pretty well drove the class. I decided early on that I was going to be an active participant in class. For one thing, that was a good insurance policy. If you spoke up often in class the professor would know who you were and whether you did your homework and whether you had anything to say and how well you could say it. If you had a bad exam day, you probably weren't sunk.

Another even more persuasive reason to participate fully in class was that that was the way to get the most out of that first year. Each class became a little puzzle for the students—or whichever students were really taking part that day, to solve. Spending five or six hours a day in that intellectual pressure cooker of bright students was a truly thrilling experience.

It will come as no surprise to learn that the vast majority of MBA students at Harvard were ambitious. A major subject of conversation related to what was next. I was quite taken aback by the extent to which how much money could be made at this or that endeavor dominated the debate. I was undecided, but the more I learned about the world of business, via the parade of case studies that filled our waking hours, the clearer it became that I needed an activity that had something other than the bottom line as its motivator. In addition, our long wedding trip had sharpened our already strong interest in work with at least a strong international component. I looked at many general areas of interest, but my thoughts regularly returned to the United States Foreign Service. If you wanted to work abroad in the field of foreign affairs, why not do it in the most direct way? Join the U.S. Foreign Service.

Entrance into the Foreign Service is by examination. There was an oral exam that some 30 percent of applicants passed; I didn't worry about that hurdle. Getting into the Foreign Service was very competitive, even back then, but the chokepoint was the oral exam, not the written. The received wisdom was that pretty well everyone from a highly selective school like St. Paul's and Harvard passed the written. Moreover, I tested well. I got into Harvard not based on my good grades in secondary school but mostly on my SAT scores. So with a light heart I took the test and was both flabbergasted and crestfallen to learn I had failed it. I had known I had had a bad day, and had spent way too much time on one section of the exam, but to fail? The only saving grace was that I could take it again. I could even make a virtue out of necessity by putting the year that I lost by failing the test to good use by taking a one-year master's degree program in Foreign Affairs at the Fetcher School of Law and Diplomacy, a foreign affairs school administered jointly by Harvard and Tufts.

In June of 1960, Louisa and I both put on our rented caps and gowns and graduated from Harvard and Radcliffe, I with an MBA and Louisa with a BA. Dad, who had never really forgiven me for having allowed our wedding day to coincide with—and take precedence over—my (he thought partly his) Harvard graduation, was thereby able to attend at least one of his son's graduation ceremonies.

For the Fletcher year, we continued to live in our little house on Rice Street which could barely accommodate our growing family. Nicholas, son two, arrived in September of 1959, at the fall term of Louisa's senior year. (Louisa announced that Nicholas was her undergraduate thesis.) She graduated with honors in general studies.

During my Fletcher year, Louisa contented herself with raising the boys and having Eliza in May 1961, just in time for my Fletcher graduation. We doted on our two boys, but were thrilled to add a girl to our family. Moreover, she turned out to be a well-behaved young lady, even as an infant.

▄▄▄▄

Suddenly, however, I was no longer in school. The long-running question that had so terrified me when we were young marrieds: "What's Bill going to do?" plagued me anew. But we had decided what we would like if we could make it work. I would join the Foreign Service. During the Fletcher year I had re-taken the written exam again and done well. The first one, which I had failed, had been an aberration, I argued. It happens sometimes. We were still in Cambridge and the oral exam was only given in Washington. I scheduled it and on the appointed day, flew down.

Three Foreign Service Officers made up every panel. The word was that they would have agreed beforehand which role each would play—the heavy, the good guy, and a don't-give-a-damn member. I have known many officers who have served as examiners and they have unanimously and vehemently denied that or anything like it exists. Perhaps. But it certainly happened in my case. One jolly, chubby guy went way out of his way to give me the benefit of the doubt. Another didn't like anything about me and made no effort to conceal that. The last had no interest in being part of the proceeding—what he wanted to do, and did, was read his *New York Times* on the sly.

My exam started badly. I just plain drew a blank on a question that was not even a real question but a device to begin a conversation. Question: "What holiday in France corresponds to our Fourth of July?" Answer: "the 14th of July, Bastille Day." Except that I couldn't come up with that to save my soul. I was reminded of a story a classmate of mine at Fletcher told about his own oral exam. He got a softball like mine, whose purpose really was just to get things going. Question: "What do you think of the Transcendentalists?" He, too, drew a blank and couldn't think of an idea or a person to identify with the movement. His answer: "It's a very interesting movement." That just dug him in farther and farther until it was too late. He failed. It didn't help that he was married to the daughter of one of our best known and respected diplomats.

In my case, my nemesis latched onto the idea that what not coming up with Bastille Day showed was that I was entirely ignorant about labor movements, at home and abroad. My problem was that in fact, I was pretty weak in the whole area. I might have been sunk if the good guy hadn't come to my aid. "I think we have established Mr. Newlin needs to brush up on his labor movements. Let us go on and determine whether this weakness is isolated or typical." Then I got a break. My enemy fancied himself strong in the economic area and he went after me. Happily, fresh from a Harvard MBA and all the economics Fletcher had to offer I was playing from strength. Even better, he had no one to get him to drop that line of questioning and try to find my weakness so he continued for nearly the rest of the time probing for weakness in my strongest subject and one in which I outshone him. In his last five minutes, he tried me on books. Did I read very much? "Pretty much," I answered, "I like books." Luck was with me again. If Louisa, who knows every book I have read in the last ten years, if not in my life, had picked the books, she couldn't have done better. Every book he picked was one I knew something about. Many were ones about which I could talk happily at length. At last the exam was over and the panel filed out to confer. The deal was they would give me thumbs up or down right there. As I waited for them to return with the verdict, I decided if I failed I would not take it again. I had been lucky this time. Most of the time had been spent on my strongest area and the books that had been picked gave me my best chance.

Then they came back. The bad guy spoke first. "It's remarkable you have gotten as far as you have in life without a better grounding in the world's labor movements." He really spit this out, disgusted with me. "That's it," I thought. "I've flunked. No Foreign Service for us." I hated the prospect of telling Louisa. She had quite warmed to the idea of being a diplomat's wife. "Don't get the wrong idea," the good guy chimed in. "We want you in the Foreign Service and we hope you will accept our invitation; but we do expect you to bone up on the labor movement."

I was in. There was a lot of bureaucratic work ahead, but the big beautiful truth was that I was about to join the United States Foreign Service.

I found a phone booth and called Louisa, who was delighted. I then took a cab to National Airport, where I had a couple of celebratory double bourbons before boarding my flight home to Boston.

## 8

# DRINKING LUNCH
# IN PARIS

WE HAD EXPECTED TO STAY IN WASHINGTON FOR our first tour. We had figured most of our class would be eager to go abroad, so there would be little competition for the available slots in Washington. We had even bought a comfortable white frame house in Cleveland Park, the closest thing we could find in Washington to Brattle Street in Cambridge. I remember sitting in the large auditorium as the officer in charge of our training class made a little drama over announcing the assignments. My colleagues were being assigned all over the world, some to big posts: Tokyo, Manila, Cairo, Argentina; some to obscure ones: Bamako, Mamama, Matamoros, Guangzhou. When he called my name, he made a little game of pretending not being able to read the assignment, puzzling over it as if trying to figure it out. "It's pronounced Ouagadougou," I prompted him.

"No," he said, "It's pronounced Paris." And so it was.

Louisa was initially disappointed at our not having the couple of years we had counted on to settle into our new house. Our little family had been growing. Nick was two already and an impish bundle of energy, and Eliza, our smiling little girl, had just been born. Louisa had her hands full. But the prospect of going to Paris, which she remembered so fondly from our honeymoon days, soon brought her around. Getting our fifty-year-old house, and our young family, ready to go to Paris with only a couple of months' notice, and the trip there on the *Queen Mary*— first class thanks to your tax dollars—is a story of its own. So was finding an apartment and getting the family settled in Paris. Louisa brilliantly bore the brunt of the moving operation both in Washington and in Paris. I don't remember alcohol playing much of a role in these activities.

At a dinner party I had met Ed Dale, a senior economics reporter for *The New York Times*. He was interested in learning of my imminent assignment to Paris, and undertook to write a note about my arrival to his close friend Jacques Reinstein, the economic minister and third highest-ranking officer in the embassy after the ambassador and his deputy. Reinstein took me to lunch the very day I arrived. He was desperate. His deputy had just moved on and Reinstein needed help. He put me to work that same afternoon, so within hours of my arrival, I found myself as the assistant, sounding board, and confidant of the man dealing with the issue of the day—the formation of the European Common Market—and the United States' role in the new Europe. I called Louisa at the Hôtel des Deux Mondes, the embassy-owned hotel in which she, I, Billy, Nick, Eliza, and our bassett hound Falstaff had been ensconced and told her I had a job and big office with a fireplace overlooking the Place de la Concorde. My foreign service career was launched.

Falling into Reinstein's lap had been a stroke of great good fortune. Typically, junior officers in Paris went directly to the consular office, where they spent most of their time rotating between issuing visas and passports and back again. I had escaped that fate. But had going to Paris subjected me to a totally unanticipated danger? It was the dream assignment from a substantive standpoint, but it had exposed me to a danger from an entirely unanticipated quarter—lunch. What got me in trouble in Paris was not the boredom of an uninteresting assignment—it was long lunch breaks.

The American Embassy was in a classy, bustling section of Paris full of shops and offices. At midday, office workers of all stripes poured into the streets in need of a good lunch. In the 1960s, it was still true that you could not get a bad meal in Paris. My idea of heaven was to join that hungry French crowd at its national pastime: déjeuner. This I usually did alone.

There was an embassy cafeteria which served pretty good fare, and lots of embassy personnel, including my junior officer colleagues, ate there. I would often join them, especially at first. For one thing, it was a good bargain. But that wasn't my idea of being in Paris. More and more, when I didn't have to eat with my boss—which I had to do any time he did not already have a lunch date—I chose to eat alone, at one of the little local restaurants.

These were simple establishments. Decor was minimal, a few pictures on the walls. The chairs were no-nonsense and the tables had stiff white paper over the tablecloths. The paper was changed between customers, but not the cloth. You did get a cloth napkin, but you were charged a small cover—*couvert*—for that luxury and for your cutlery. In some restaurants, cubbyholes were still in evidence where regular customers used to store their napkins between meals and therefore avoid the cover charge, but alas, by 1962 the practice had fallen into disuse.

The menu was basic. Simple starters were offered like *radis au beurre, céleri rémoulade,* or *paté campagne.* Staples of the main course menu were the basics: *steak frites, sole meunière,* or *escalope de veau.* Dessert might be *mousse au chocolat* or a crème caramel. For me, more tempting at the end would be the *plateau de fromage.* You got your choice of three; I would get a blue, like Roquefort or Bleu de Bresse, a soft cheese like a Camembert or Brie, and a mild, hard cheese like a Gruyère or an Emmenthal.

I talk about the food, and it was the centerpiece, but more central to my story is the wine that went with it. Nearly all customers took wine, and most stuck with a quarter liter carafe—*un quart*—but early on that didn't seem like quite enough for me. At the very least, I found I would need a second *quart de rouge* to go with the cheese. And as time passed and I settled into my new life, sometimes even a third *quart* seemed like a very nice way to finish off the meal. The basic white wine in Paris then was a Muscadet and for years, a sip of Muscadet would bring me back to déjeuner, circa 1962. The red was more nondescript, at least to my palate.

Reinstein liked me, and, more to the point, he needed me. He was that sort who couldn't be alone. I was his sounding board. He would talk and I would listen. In the office he would not read anything I had not read first. I screened his in-box and put things in order, often affixing little notes calling particular items to his attention. I would attend all meetings he had with his own staff, and he would often bring me with him to meetings in other parts of the embassy. After these he would want a little note with my impressions of what important happened. He was a brilliant man, but he was a poor communicator. Often after a meeting with his subordinates, one or more of them would call or come by to talk to me. "What the hell did he say? What in the world does he want?" Often, because of remarks Reinstein had made to me before or after the meeting, I could tell them. Sometimes I was baffled, too, but I could more easily ask him for clarification than they.

It was a good period. I was doing useful work, and I was learning a lot about our economic relations with Europe. The Common Market was being born, and how it would interface with the US was not yet clear. Reinstein had great insights, but they were at odds with what Washington wanted to hear. The exchange across the ocean was fascinating, particularly seeing how stubbornly the Washington side clung to its views that despite evidence to the contrary, the new Europe would not do violence to basic U.S. interests. I also learned a lot about how the embassy worked.

I was on thin ice with my drinking, however. I am now, as I remember being then, reminded of the character in *Bartleby the Scrivener* who regularly came back to his desk red faced after a long lunch and was prone to blotting his copy book in the afternoons. He did it literally. I feared I might be doing it figuratively. I could tell sometimes that I wasn't doing my best work after lunch. Reinstein still appeared to value me and rely on me, but did he harbor doubts? It was with some trepidation that I opened my first Foreign Service annual evaluation. I was relieved to read: "It has been a long time since I have encountered a Foreign Service Officer as attractive and talented as Mr. Newlin." So once more, I was getting away with it. On three quarters of a liter of wine, I was probably legally drunk when I came back from a particularly liquid lunch, but my boss still liked how I was doing my job. Like the gingerbread man in the children's folk tale, who always runs just a little faster than his pursuers, I had a knack for staying just one step ahead of trouble. But, as we shall see, trouble is persistent.

I have explained how in principle, first year officers rotate throughout the embassy, getting a feel of how things are done by spending three- and four-month tours in each department. I had been in Reinstein's office for a little over a year and the Personnel office was beginning to take notice. Reinstein, they argued, couldn't keep Newlin forever. Reinstein was willing to play fair and relinquish me, but only on his terms. He asked that they assign me to the U.S. Mission to the North Atlantic Treaty Organization (NATO), stationed just outside of Paris. There, he argued, I would get exposed to a whole new command structure and new issues which would be much better training for me than any new assignment in the embassy proper. He won out and they sent me to NATO headquarters.

Reinstein was right; it was an entirely different sort of operation. I was assigned to work under John Auchincloss, then head of the Political office. Auchincloss was an old line Foreign Service officer and gentleman who believed in the mentor system. Young officers learned from old timers. He, too, took me under his wing, but we had a very different relationship from the one I had enjoyed with Reinstein. Auchincloss didn't need me. He saw his role as being there to help me. He assigned me to "follow" the big issue of the day, the Multilateral Force. This was a scheme beloved of the U.S. ambassador to NATO at the time, Thomas Finletter, under which the naval side of NATO would consist of ships manned by a mix of NATO nationalities. It was designed to get around the French opposition to American dominance of the NATO navy. The political and practical opposition to this whole idea was massive, and the idea never got off the ground, but it was the hot topic during the spring of 1964 when I was there. Auchincloss made sure I was invited to all meetings dealing with the issue, and when he couldn't get me in on my own, he would send me to represent him.

It was interesting as much as an example of an exercise in futility as for anything else. It was clear to me that the whole idea was misguided. If it ever came into being, it wouldn't work, but that was moot because there was no way the French would let it happen. In the end, the French not only scuttled the Multilateral Force idea, but they pulled all French troops out of the NATO unified command entirely, and then they threw the NATO command out of Paris. The entire episode was a high stakes game for a junior Foreign Service officer at his first posting.

From a drinking standpoint, the setup in the NATO was altogether different from in Paris. The NATO headquarters were outside Paris in a self-contained enclave. There was no eating lunch in little local bistros. People ate in the central cafeteria. Moreover, Auchincloss saw to it that I used my lunch periods to get to know the rest of the U.S. delegation and the key people in the other delegations. He would quiz me on my lunchtime activities.

I only remember one occasion during that NATO period when drink nearly caught up with me. A senior delegation was sent from Washington for some high-level meetings. I was to meet them at the airport. I went out with a couple of embassy cars to bring them in. Like a good scout, I arranged to get there in plenty of time. My early arrival gave me time for a drink in the bar—and then another. But they were late. I had another. By the time they arrived, I'd had more than I had intended. Often it was hard for me to tell how much my having drunk too much showed. I was able to realize I was more gone than was normal even for me, but no one made any sign of seeing that anything was out of the ordinary. The next morning the delegation was all smiles and Auchincloss was his usual cordial self. I had been given another pass.

I soon tired of the NATO assignment. I felt that in the area we were spending most of our political capital, the Multilateral Force, we were wasting our time. I was also running out of time. There were just a few months left in my Paris time and the Personnel office was after me again. I still had not spent any time at all in the consular section; they insisted on their pound of flesh.

With just two months to go, I was sentenced to crank out non-immigrant visas. I'm a good sport; they caught me fair and square and I went uncomplainingly. In fact, my short visa interlude proved remarkably satisfying. The vast majority of those who joined the Foreign Service with me were convinced we were destined to create a better world. The official title for what we were joining was the Foreign Service, but we all knew we were joining the *diplomatic corps*—which to us had much more panache.

I doubt if any of us had even thought of something as prosaic as the Consular Corps. Whatever that was, it wouldn't affect us diplomats. Yet here I was in the Visa Section and the very lowest man on the totem pole.

I was trained by my peers, junior officers who had preceded me to that duty. In those days, getting a tourist visa from France wasn't hard. As long as you had no problems with crimes of "moral turpitude," and had steered clear of the Communist Party, all you had to show was that you "had a residence abroad you had no intention of abandoning," and that you were not "likely to become a public charge." In other words, you didn't plan on emigrating to the US and you were not going to go on our welfare rolls.

In 1964 tourists were flocking to the US for vacation, and the Commerce Department had a whole division promoting such travel. We wanted their money. One large and lucrative tourist sub-category was French students wanting to go to America for summer vacation. In the spring, when I began my visa stint, the waiting room of the Visa Section was clogged with bright, eager French students applying for their visas. These would-be friends of America thought they were beginning their trip to our shores by having to clear a pesky bureaucratic hurdle. In fact, they were about to discover themselves bogged down in a messy, cumbersome, bureaucratic swamp.

The attitude of my predecessors towards granting visas seemed to be "If you can slow 'em down, do so." To establish that they did not intend to stay in the US, the student applicants had to produce a fist-full of papers demonstrating their intention to return to France. Students were encouraged to bring such documents as round-trip tickets, school enrollment forms, or even letters from family or prominent French citizens attesting to the student's likely return at the end of the summer. Notarized documents counted double. Students were routinely refused their visa on the first visit on grounds of insufficient documentation.

Applicants also had to prove financial responsibility. They had to have enough money to spend a summer in the US without going broke and seeking help from U.S. public sources. (Imagine a vacationing French student subjecting himself to a U.S. welfare office!) Someone had determined that $400 was enough to finance an American summer, so the applicant had to show he was good for at least that amount.

I considered those requirements to be ridiculous. In the first place, very few French students in 1964 had the slightest desire to emigrate to America. But more importantly, if one actually wanted to do so, these silly requirements would do no more than slow them down. Even the most inept student would be able to obtain a collection of documents demonstrating intention to return to France at the end of the summer. The $400 requirement was an even bigger joke. Many applicants satisfied it by showing that amount in ready money. What matter if the same wad of bills was passed around from student to student? It was only necessary to have it in your possession for five minutes; you didn't have to own it. So the primary result of making the visa requirements for students burdensome was just to clog the waiting room, which engendered ill will among the students.

Then, just two weeks after my arrival in the Visa Section, serendipity struck. All the "old timers" rotated out en masse, and a new batch of junior officers replaced them. This made me the ranking officer among those actually giving visas. There was no glory or prestige to being the head of the Non-Immigrant Visa Section, but it did give me the obligation—and opportunity—to train the newcomers.

I told them that non-immigrant visa officers should have two primary goals in their dealings with students: 1) Move them along just as fast as possible, and 2) Make sure their first contact with official America was a pleasure. We wanted them to go into the world and say in surprised wonder: "I just got my visa for the US and it was a snap—even kind of fun."

The new batch of officers was only too glad to operate under these guidelines and in no time we had cut to a fraction the waiting time for a U.S. tourist visa. An unintended consequence of the clearer waiting room was that we could make a little ceremony surrounding any such illustrious visa-seekers we encountered. In my two-month span in the Visa Section, I had the fun of giving visas to Maurice Chevalier (going on a tour), Rex Harrison (going to make *My Fair Lady*), and as the crowning visa moment, giving visas to all four Beatles (coming on their first U.S. tour.) We decided to limit our autograph hunting to only one randomly chosen supplicant who would ask for one full set.

Happily, the winner was our most comely Foreign Service National employee, who was a big hit with the band.

Once back in the heart of Paris, I went back to my old liquid lunch habits, except that visa office lunches were more brief than political and economic section ones, so I was obliged to forego the third *quart de rouge* for the cheese. Working for either Reinstein or at NATO, what I felt I had to protect against was being caught not able to function well enough to carry my weight. In both Reinstein's office and in NATO you were never very far away from the substance of diplomacy. Most conversation related to work. How should we reply to the community's new proposals on the common agricultural tariff? Who in the French delegation might tip his hand on the French position on this or that? I always had to be in a position to have views on any topic, and be able to defend them.

Work in the Visa Section was different. For one thing, for all practical purposes, I never saw my boss. He sat in his office and heaven alone knows what he did. In my experience, visa officers on the line were never observed by their supervisors as they performed their duties. No one ever sat in on a single one of my visa interviews. That clearly took some of the pressure off. The people who would write my performance ratings never saw me work, drunk or sober. But another factor made an even greater difference in the way I looked at my drinking in the two work settings.

What visa officers did was interview the public. I always thought a good interview contained a touch of the theatrical. I considered dishing out American charm to be part of the job. I wanted applicants to go away with a smile on their face; the jolly visa guy was the one to put it there. When I came back from lunch a bit jollier than the next guy, I persuaded myself that a little moderate drinking enhanced my ability to give a good interview. I never thought that in my "real" jobs.

One incident during this period scared me. Deprived of my third *quart* with the cheese, I sometimes stopped for a quick *vin blanc* on the way home. Our work stopped when we shut the doors and in the visa office it was considered entirely acceptable to go right home. (In the substantive offices the unwritten law was that junior officers hung around as long as their bosses—and senior officers had a weakness for long hours). One night, however, I had to stay late at the visa office finishing up a report. It was nearly eight when I left. I had warned Louisa I would be late and she had put the kids to bed, so I was in no hurry. Walking to the Metro, tired, I stopped at a café for a little pick-me-up. I encountered, to my surprise, a fellow officer, a somewhat pathetic specimen named Denis. He had started home an hour and a half before me, but he was still there at the bar. We talked a little and it came out this was his routine. He would stop off, always in the same corner of the same café, for an hour—or even two—before going home. He had drunk too much—so much he slurred his words a little. He was falling over the edge that I was trying so hard to avoid. Drunks are rare in the State Department. I never met another Denis—nor, for that matter, another me

I realized in a horrible moment that was where I would be heading if I didn't watch out. I saw, as I had never previously, that what I was doing had two risks. Beyond the risk of being found out to be drinking more than was acceptable lay a second, more pernicious danger. I could end up like Denis. That realization didn't stop me drinking. That insight probably didn't even slow me down much. But the image of lonely, pathetic, drunk Denis at the bar haunted me for years.

I had lots of faults, but dallying on the way home wasn't one of them. I liked the home front; I loved being with my family. When I was with Reinstein and at NATO we worked late as a rule, and I had to hurry home if I was going to get to see the children at all. A plus of working at the Visa Section was that I got home earlier and had more time with them.

Home early or late, I got to see my children in the old-fashioned way, from the perspective of a traditional dad whose parenting was heavy on fun and light on work. Bill, Nick, and Eliza, then ages 7, 5, and 3, were presented to me bathed, fed, and ready to play. Their pleasure at my arrival was always uplifting. I still see their happy faces crying "Daddy" as they ran towards me. We would play, have a read, and watch a magical five-minute TV segment during which Grand Nou' Nourse (Big Teddy Bear) would send children all over France scurrying to their beds with fairy dust and *"Bonne nuit, les petits."* Only after they were down would Louisa and I have our dinner.

It's easy to forget what a handful three kids under five are. We had a Canadian girl who helped Louisa at the beginning, and then a young French woman who stayed with us the whole time, and in fact came back to Washington with us, but it was still a handful—easily a two-person job. Remember, we are talking about Paris in the mid-sixties. One did not shop at a supermarket. One took one's string bag to a variety of specialty shops, the butcher, the baker, and the candlestick maker. It was having that extra help that allowed us to have a somewhat civilized, grown-up dinner hour. For me, that meant a drink and a dividend every night, perhaps a plate of cheese and crackers, and some wine with dinner. Remember the cocktail hour? Here we were upholding standards.

My impression of the Paris years is that while my drinking was still not a major issue between Louisa and me, there was always some tension with Louisa putting the brakes on my consumption. For example, in a restaurant where wine was served by the bottle, I always thought a good meal rated a whole bottle. Louisa, who often would only have one or at most two glasses, thought we could get away with a half. In simple restaurants where we would often order wine by the carafe, she naturally plugged for a half carafe, I a whole. Sometimes we did it my way, sometimes hers.

Sometimes I would have so much to drink that others could see I had had too much. That was always upsetting to Louisa. I remember one occasion at a reception at the apartment of a good friend of Louisa's. My condition reached the point that the guest of honor remarked to our hostess that one of the guests appeared to have had too much to drink. I was taken home in disgrace. On another occasion, we went out to dinner with a couple passing through Paris on their way to somewhere where the gentleman was going to settle down and write the great American novel. That made me jealous, so I drank too much to the point that I had a little nap in the restaurant loo. Incidents like these were mortifying to Louisa, and going out knowing that they could occur could spoil her pleasure. But it did not happen very often. Louisa hated these mortifying incidents but managed to forget them quickly.

Louisa, of course, did not know the extent of my lunchtime drinking, but once, we ate together in one of the restaurants in which I would often have three little *quarts*.

One of the waiters made some jocular reference to the fact that I was being particularly abstemious that day in front of the little woman. Louisa picked up on it and queried me. I tried to make light of the incident, but I am sure the remark registered with Louisa, and was upsetting.

The Paris time came to an end. We returned to Washington on the U.S.S. *United States* with our three now bilingual children, and with a love for France and especially Paris that is still with us. I had successfully completed my first assignment as a diplomat and got high praise from the three rating officers under whom I had served. Those ratings served me well at the next ranking period when I was promoted, one of a small number of those in my class so favored that soon. But I had picked up a very bad habit—that of lunching alone, and drinking too much at lunch. That practice caught up with me at my next Washington posting.

# 9

# BROUGHT LOW IN WASHINGTON

FROM PARIS, IN AUGUST, 1964, I WAS ASSIGNED back to Washington, to the Economic Bureau and an assignment in the Office of Trade Agreements. The US was preparing for what was known as the Kennedy Round of tariff negotiations, and there was much to be done.

From a personal standpoint, coming home to Washington was great for the family. We had bought our house before leaving and had rented it to a French admiral during our absence. We owned it, but had never lived in it. This would give us a chance to get to know our house and our city. Moreover, I was pleased with my new job. I still thought I would to be able to parlay my business school education into a career on the political side of the Foreign

Service, with a strong economic slant. I thought the Kennedy Round would give me a chance to make a mark.

One of the functions of the Trade Agreements office was to act as a liaison with other parts of the government engaged in preparing our positions for the ongoing negotiations in Geneva. These interagency planning meetings in Washington would typically take place in the early afternoon. I can still quite clearly remember the very meeting that did me in. It was an interagency gathering presided over by a senior member of the Office of the President's Special Representative for Trade Negotiations (STR). The object of the meeting was to divide up the tasks that each agency would take on in preparing the position papers for our negotiators. Looking back, it seems quite remarkable that I was representing the State Department at this meeting, at this level. I was new to the department, just back from my first tour overseas. In that room were seasoned representatives of the Departments of Commerce, Treasury, Agriculture, Labor, and Defense, and who knows who else. I really had no inkling how Washington worked then, or how all these agencies interacted.

Inexperience was not my only problem. When I knew I was going to be at a meeting where I would be a bit out of my depth, I took to fortifying myself beforehand by lunching at one of the local restaurants that served booze. My drink of choice was bourbon on the rocks; at my favorite restaurant, just around the corner from my office, they were served in miniatures. Two miniatures contained three ounces of bourbon, a great source of strength in interagency meetings.

So at this particular meeting, fortified by three ounces of bourbon at lunch, I didn't feel out of my depth at all. I knew the score. Pieces of the pie were being sliced up and given away. The commodities were going to the agencies that dealt with them. Agriculture got the crops. Commerce got manufactured products. Defense would deal with weaponry. There were some pieces, such as shipping, that crossed commodities borders and that everyone seemed to agree fell to State. But there was one piece that no one seemed to want: pulp and paper. There was no volunteer, and no consensus as to where it fell. Hell, I thought, that can't be hard; I haven't got a real piece yet—I'll protect State's turf and grab pulp and paper for us. And I did. And no one seemed to think that was unreasonable. Back in my office, I reported what had transpired, that I had volunteered to do the position paper on pulp and paper and no one seemed to think one way or the other about it.

OK, so I was going to handle the U.S. government's position paper on pulp and paper. The problem was that I didn't have the slightest idea how to go about preparing such a position. I had never seen such a document or anything close to it. The person in our office I thought had a good command of the office's files didn't, but it wouldn't have helped, because the files contained nothing useful about pulp and paper anyway. The library wasn't much more use. I was really in a quandary, and my boss wasn't the slightest help. He didn't know what to do either, so he distanced himself from the issue completely. Newlin was doing pulp and paper, not he.

My solution was not the most salutary. I took to lunching alone nearly every day, and I upped my bourbon intake from one or two miniatures per lunch to three and sometimes even four. My afternoons were spent massaging figures relating to the pulp and paper industry in interesting but entirely unconstructive ways. There would be periodic bleats from the negotiating team in Geneva: Were they going to get any guidance on pulp and paper? Sometimes they would come up with specific questions, and those I could usually handle. I was acquiring some familiarity with the data. But I never did get a grip on what the overall U.S. position should be, and I never came close to producing a comprehensive document.

Then, I made a real tactical blunder. I was presented with the perfect out and I didn't take it. I don't know to what extent drinking clouded my judgment on this point. My potential salvation came in the form of a call from the executive assistant to the Assistant Secretary for Economic Affairs. It seemed the Assistant Secretary needed a new assistant and I had been recommended; he was offering me the job. It would be a feather in my cap. The executive assistant jobs were plums, given to up-and-coming young officers. But I turned it down. Just days earlier, I had had a long conversation at dinner with an officer a few years ahead of me who had done quite a bit of "front office" staff work, and he was sounding off about how shallow that was compared to having your own slice of "substantive" work. No amount of staff work could equal being the decision maker on an issue. Better to have your own slice of the pie than a staff role involving bigger slices. I had agreed with him, and the two of us had defended that position against another officer who was making his mark on the senior staff side. How could I now abandon my substantive piece of the action in favor of a staff position? When I reported my decision to the Assistant Secretary, he certainly seemed surprised, and even a bit deflated, but he didn't press me.

The more I think about that decision in retrospect, the more fateful it seems. Had I taken the executive assistant slot, several beautiful things would have happened. First and foremost, the whole pulp and paper burden would have simply been lifted from me. That alone would have been worth anything. But even more importantly, I think it would have at least delayed some of my drinking problems. As it was, pulp and paper continued to be my millstone, and the clever way I handled it was to get a buzz on at lunch that would last me through the afternoon. Had I accepted the executive assistant job, liquid lunches would have been impossible, and my descent into spending my afternoons in an alcoholic haze would have at least been postponed.

As it was, that was my most painful period in the State Department, and one of the periods during which I came the closest to losing control. I was always a "well-compensated" alcoholic, but during my time at Trade Agreements, I drank so much it is hard to see how I avoided being exposed. But I wasn't. For much of those two years, I produced no work of any value and no supervisor ever really challenged me. That was, and still is, inexplicable to me, and speaks nearly as badly for the department as it does for me. Diplomats have a reputation for heavy drinking, and this account might seem to confirm that. I want to make very clear, however, that my own behavior was, with a handful of exceptions over 25 years, totally atypical. I never encountered anyone who abused alcohol as much as I did. No one came close. Quite to the contrary, I found my colleagues to be hard working and abstemious. Did my supervisors and colleagues know I was drinking too much and turn a blind eye? Did they never smell alcohol on my breath? Or did they simply think I was underperforming? I have never known.

## 10

# SNEAKING DRINKS
# IN GUATEMALA

THE WAY THE DEPARTMENT'S ASSIGNMENT REGIME worked in the mid-sixties was that typically a new officer's first three assignments consisted of a Washington tour, and two tours overseas, each in different parts of the world. I had served in Paris and Washington; it was time for something foreign, outside of Europe. You got to ask for whatever you wanted, but you took whatever you were given. I can't remember what I asked for, but I was given Guatemala.

We didn't know much about Guatemala, but knew it was called the "Land of Eternal Spring," which had to count for something. We would live in Guatemala City, at about 5,000 feet, surrounded by high mountains, colonial cities, indigenous villages and markets, and world famous ruins. That was all good. A downside was that it came with a huge gap between the rich and the poor, with the poor living in terrible urban poverty (rural poverty, too, but that's rarely quite so evident). Worse, the U.S. government was supporting an oppressive local regime that in turn supported the entrenched rich.

The trip down to Guatemala merits a book in itself. We drove from Texas to Guatemala in the summer of 1966 in our VW bus, with three children, then five, six, and nine; Felicia Sandiga, our valued Peruvian housekeeper; and our beloved springer spaniel Barkus. Felicia was to help us settle in, and help hire a staff appropriate to an American diplomat in Guatemala, where hiring "help" costs little for Americans but provides much sought-after local employment. Felicia would then visit her family in Peru, and later return to the US to become, once again, her family's breadwinner.

The trip had its problems. We had made the decision to drive down too late to line up the best hotels en route, so we were stuck with the second—or even third—string. Along the Pan-American Highway ("highway" is a misnomer if ever there was one), second string meant green water in the swimming pools and dicey food and water.

We made a big point to the children about drinking nothing but *"agua purificada,"* which could be found, we were assured by the helpful staff, in the carafes in every room. (This was long before the now-ubiquitous plastic bottles of drinking water.) The first night there, Nicholas was under the weather with an earache, and he chose to have his dinner in his room, not the dining room. While we went to get dinner that we would bring him on a tray, he had been alone in the room during the maid's evening rounds, turning down beds and the like. When we returned, Nicholas was eager to impart to us some newfound knowledge: "The water in the taps in this hotel is *purifacada*," he announced. We were horrified. "Oh no, Nicky, it's not. Do not drink it."

"It is too *purificada*," he insisted, proud of his inside knowledge, "You said the water in the carafes was *purificada* and I saw the maid fill the carafes from the tap." That was not all.

The next morning at breakfast we had pancakes, and smack in the middle of the glass syrup jar, as if preserved in amber, was a large, dead fly. Louisa was not pleased. "*Mosca*," she said, showing the fly to the waiter. The waiter joined right in on the game. "*Sí*," he said, "*mosca*," pleased to confirm the American lady's correct Spanish vocabulary. We did manage to have the syrup and its *mosca* removed, and replaced with a *mosca*-less syrup pitcher, but we all knew it was the same pitcher, simply sans *mosca*.

It was a long ride, which took us on dirt roads, through sleepy, dusty villages, around hairpin turns on steep mountainsides, and through noisy city centers, with many a stop in less-than-sparkling hotels and eateries. It was nine eventful days, but the pot of gold at the end of the rainbow was the Biltmore Hotel in Guatemala City, a first-class American-style hotel with a pristine swimming pool and big, fat, juicy hamburgers. Our first night there, Nicky said with real feeling, "The Biltmore is the best hotel in the world." We all agreed.

What I liked best about the Biltmore was the bar. Bourbon was my drink of choice then, and it had been scarce or non-existent the length of the Pan-American Highway. At the Biltmore, however, bourbon on the rocks was world class. For starters, they were big. The bartender would fill the rocks glass with ice and then fill it to the brim with 100-proof bourbon. That probably made for a drink of something more than two ounces. Moreover, a drink never came without a plate of delicious snacks called *boquitas,* which at the Biltmore consisted of assorted spreads on bite-sized tortillas. We later learned that even the meanest *tienda* in *el campo* will give you something to eat, even if only a peanut or an olive, to accompany your *indita* (the cheapest, rawest alcohol).

Those big, beautiful bourbons were a magnet to me. One evening, when Louisa had her hands full getting everyone ready for bed, I contrived some reason to excuse myself briefly. To get something form the car? I don't remember. I went right to the bar, and was hurrying through my two ounces plus of bourbon, when a young American woman came into the bar like an avenging angel. She accosted a hapless guy sitting alone at a table, obviously her husband. She ripped him up and down verbally at the top of her lungs. She may have even whacked him with her purse, but I could be making that up. The gist of her harangue was what the hell did he think he was doing, getting sozzled in the bar, when she was up dealing with the kids? He had dragged her down here to this God-forsaken country from Toledo and if he didn't shape up she was going right back home. I scuttled back up to our room where I belonged without even finishing my drink.

We needed a place to live and we lucked out finding an attractive little house, available for a couple of months while the owners were on vacation. We were particularly taken by its lovely walled garden. (We later learned all gardens were walled. How else would you keep the *ladrones*— robbers—out?) It would have been too small for us in the long run, but it was great as a stopgap.

I went right to work at the embassy. Louisa's job, on top of taking care of three displaced children, was finding us a house. She nearly didn't show me the place we ended up in, because she knew I would love it and she figured we could do better. She was right on the first point. I wanted it the moment I saw it. We will never know if we could have done better, because we took it. Louisa called it the "Crazy House" and that stuck. It belonged to the first vice-president of the Guatemalan congress, and it was only available because he had been kidnapped for ransom, escaped, and had fled to the US. What made it "crazy" was the layout, and that was no problem if you accepted that the children's bedrooms were on the other side of the kitchen courtyard, far from us in the main house, and that the playroom was up a flight of stairs and away from the rest of the house. I liked it for its long wall decorated with a replica of a mural at Bonampak, a famous Mayan ruin. (We later saw a true replica of the Bonampak mural and discovered ours had been, fortunately, bowdlerized, leaving out the most bloody parts.)

The Crazy House, for all its idiosyncrasies, worked well for us, and we got lots of mileage out of its swimming pool. We, especially the kids, loved swimming in it, but not the least of its benefits was that during the dry season, we were never without water, because we could use the pool as our reservoir. Many were the elaborate and fancy dinners we attended where guests followed one another to toilets which, being without water, couldn't flush—imagine!— but this never happened at the Newlins'.

I was in the Political Section of the embassy—the one on the second floor. The one on the fourth floor, also called the Political Section, was the domain of the CIA. This arrangement was widely known in Guatemala. When I said I worked in the Political Section, it was not unusual for me to be asked if I worked on the second or the fourth floor. My particular little niche of the Political Section consisted of the insurgency and the hinterland.

Visiting the hinterland gave me the excuse, on government time and expense, to travel all over the country. Most of the time I stayed in the capital, and lived at home, but every few months I could work up a little itinerary and head out into the boondocks for a week or so. I had inherited a card file of contacts beyond the capital, but I found turnover high and I pretty much had to start from scratch wherever I went. I would arrive in a town and call on the mayor, the governor, and the heads of the political parties. I was shy at first. Who was I to drive into a town and boldly go to see the mayor? I soon learned, however, that the mayor would be in khaki pants and a work shirt and would be honored to have a visit from an American diplomat, no matter how insignificant. What I wanted to know was who was in charge? What parties were strong? Were the insurgents active in that region? I didn't know then and still don't know now how accurate my sources were. The local conservative party wanted me, and by extension the U.S. government, to believe the insurgency was strong, and the center and left wanted to downplay the role and importance of the rebels.

I don't think it mattered what I reported, because the U.S. government had its own agenda that was driving (and being driven by) the fourth floor of the embassy—the CIA. In the mid-sixties the US was obsessed with communists—all insurgents were seen as communists and should be eliminated by whatever means. The Guatemalan security forces, in bed with the CIA, were systematically slaughtering liberals in universities, the media, the labor movement and the church. The story put out by both the Guatemalan government and ours was that the killings were being conducted by communist insurgent groups, notably one called the Mano Blanco, over which no officials had any control. In fact, the vast majority of the killings were carried out by the security forces themselves, masquerading as civilians.

It was a bad time to be working for the United States government in Guatemala; we were not the good guys. It was the height of the Cold War, and the domino theory prevailed. I don't know who in the embassy knew everything that was going on between the CIA and the Guatemalan government. I don't know if even our ambassador knew "officially" the extent that the CIA was collaborating with the assassinations. Whatever the senior State Department officers did or did not know "officially," everyone in Guatemala who paid the slightest attention to what was going on knew the score: It was the Guatemalan government that was responsible for the bodies turning up all over the country.

My complicity by my silence in that time is a shame to me. I did, however, initiate the one instance when the embassy, I believe for the first and only time, flagged to the senior echelons of our government in Washington that we were complicit in this systematic slaughter. I was responding to a CIA paper written for higher-ups which explicitly blamed vigilantes for the bloodbath. When I saw that article, I went to my boss, Matt Smith, and said: "We're lying to ourselves. How can you get decent policy if you're lying to yourself?" Smith grudgingly acknowledged that I could take this on if I got our ambassador, Gordon Mein, on board.

Smith declined to accompany me, saying only: "You can go see him if you want." Mein's response, when I saw him, was essentially: "Let's write it up and see what it looks like." Mein ultimately took my two-page memo, gave it to Matt Smith, and told him to write a much longer, more philosophical account of what was going on. Predictably, Mein soon received a phone call from an assistant secretary who said: "Gordon, you've upset a lot of people in Washington with this A-13 you've sent in. Can we assume this is just the work of some junior officer who's gone off the reservation?"

This made Mein furious. The report had been sent off via Air-Gram—not telegram—a hard copy document that therefore included his signature. Mein had to go back to Washington and defend his position. He never commended me for making sure that we at least once told the truth of what was going on. But he never took me to task, either, for getting him in hot water.

Life in Guatemala was normal in some respects, but not in others. There was a big expatriate community, with a large American component, both official and private. We made wonderful friends, and had a busy social life. But there were some dramatic differences from life in a typical American suburb. There were all the standard dietary deprivations and idiosyncrasies attendant to life in a developing country—we washed our lettuce in Clorox, and stayed away from ice cream, as the milk was unpasteurized. We lived behind high walls covered in broken glass, and because labor was so cheap we had live-in servants. At the same time, armed soldiers, many of them teenagers, patrolled the streets day and night. We were at risk from stray bullets, but we were also diplomatic targets. Two members of our military mission were killed during our tour, and Ambassador Gordon Mein was assassinated the very day our family left Guatemala for good.

I don't know what it was, but something about living in Guatemala kicked my drinking up a notch. It was there that Louisa became aware that my drinking had become a real problem. One circumstance that may have pushed me over the edge was again related to lunch. In both Paris and in the department, as I have reported, I had taken to very often having lunch alone, and drinking enough during lunch to carry me well into the afternoon. But in Guatemala, it would have been awkward to not have lunch with my colleagues. If I was going to get a buzz on to help me through the afternoon, I was going to have to sneak it.

I was enabled by the fact that in Guatemala City little *indigena*-run *tiendas* dotted nearly every block. They were literally just holes in the wall with a counter to put a drink on and a shelf for booze, cigarettes—which could be bought singly—and Chiclets. The booze they proffered was perfect for my purposes: *indita*, a clear vodka-like drink, served neat in a little glass right at the counter at which you stood, or sometimes, even better, in very small, flat bottles that held about four ounces. That's a great size for the secret drinker. You can even carry that around unnoticed in your pocket and have a swig at your convenience. While it was hard to lunch alone, it was easy to take a little solitary post-lunch walk to get some air or do an errand, or even pop into a washroom. A quick stop for a glug from a bottle of *indita* was easily managed.

In Paris and even in Washington, my daytime drinking was such that when I came back to the office after work I was not able to work at my best level, but I could still function. Sometimes in Guatemala, that was barely the case. Sometimes I would just go into my office and spend the rest of the afternoon not doing anything. I would shuffle paper around my desk, and read the newspaper. I was charged with compiling a weekly report about the body count found around the country, and other violence that looked political. Much of my raw material was from the press, so reading the paper was a form of "working" for me. And yet, sometimes I would hide a Spanish-language mystery novel behind the paper and read it instead. I said to myself that this was good for my Spanish. All the while I would take a little nip from time to time, from one of my little bottles just to keep feeling "right."

One reason I could get away with this was that I had a completely non-directive boss. He was pretty good at one part of his job. He was Spanish/English bilingual—he had grown up in Matamoras—and his strength was taking Guatemalan political figures to lunch, picking their brain, and writing up insightful memoranda of these conversations. What he didn't do well was supervise the output of his staff. In addition to me, there was a labor officer who kept pretty good tabs on the labor movement, but as he was keeping a pretty low profile in order to survive, he didn't have a whole lot to report. A third guy covered the parliament, but parliaments don't have much power in dictatorships so he didn't do very much either. Looking back on it, I wasn't the only one not doing a good day's work.

My boss didn't pay much attention to what any of us were doing, but I also had a secretary. It has always been hard for me to believe that she didn't realize what was going on—that her boss was pretty much in the bag many afternoons, but if she knew, she kept mum.

And of course I had Louisa. We still had a nightly cocktail hour, and while I ostensibly restricted myself to two drinks, I poured them with a heavy hand and often would be able to take a little surreptitious swig right from the bottle. When we went out to dinner, or had people over to the Crazy House, I was unreliable. It was always a crapshoot to see if I would be able to keep my drinking in check, or if I would overdo it. When I did overdo it, however, mostly I wasn't outrageous, and there was apt to be someone at the function who had had more to drink than me—or who showed it more. We had some pretty hard-drinking friends in the local expat community. But of course, Louisa could tell. She could always tell, and my drinking became a major issue between us—and was getting worse.

One day she found me drinking at the office. She had come to town for some errand or other, and had dropped by the embassy to tell me something. She realized I was in the bag the moment she walked into my office. She quickly saw that I was reading a mystery book behind my newspaper, and that I had a little bottle of *indita* in my open drawer.

She didn't say much. She scooped the incriminating evidence into her pocketbook, took me by the elbow, and with only a perfunctory word about sickness to my secretary, she whisked me home. Both my secretary and the labor attaché had not only observed that little drama, but had also seen my barely concealed slack behavior afternoon after afternoon. They never said a word to me. As far as I know, they never said a word to anyone. I wonder if they remarked on it to one another.

Louisa was, of course, furious, but also scared. What was she going to do with an alcoholic husband and three children under eleven in Guatemala? Or anywhere else, for that matter?

I was contrite, of course. That was one of my tricks, I did contrite well. I reported to work the next morning as if nothing had happened, and no one said a word. But something *had* happened.

Until now I have been mostly talking about my quiet, under-the-radar drinking, but my vice had another side. I was also, sometimes, a binge drinker. When I was drinking surreptitiously in the daytime, often I was in good control of how much I had. It's not that I could have stopped drinking, or even cut back; I couldn't. But I had a fair handle on what I took in, and I could mostly stick within my limits. In social situations, however, I was becoming increasingly unpredictable.

It did not help that there was a lively party side to Guatemala, with a handful of jolly expat partiers at its core. It was a scene I found hard to handle. I could not easily go to a party where Carlos Weissenberg was holding court and not have at least a little too much to drink myself. Carlos was a bigger-than-life partygoer, good-looking, with a nearly omnipresent broad, toothy grin, and long, wavy, black hair, an outgoing charmer who liked to be the center of attention. He bragged that he was a three time loser: a dark-skinned Latino Jew. Maybe it was making up for some of that that prompted him to be the one to arrive late at the party with the mariachi band in tow. I wasn't trying to keep up with Carlos, but when he was around, there was a lot of drinking, and Bill Newlin certainly wasn't going to be the party pooper.

Up until the *indita* incident at work, Louisa was, I think, not aware of the extent of my quiet, daily drinking. Then, it was the "too much at the party" side of my drinking that was causing her the most grief. When she dressed up to go out, she never knew which Bill would be taking her home. It was this aspect of my drinking that picked up the most in Guatemala. It became the norm, not the exception, that I would drink too much at a party. Some, people, places, or things were apt to trigger my boozing. For example, it was hard for me not to get at least a little bit drunk at a weekend luncheon at "The Castle." This was a fanciful stone imitation castle on the banks of Lake Atitlán that was rented by a bunch of rather rowdy expats, including the aforementioned Carlos. Their weekend luncheons were infamous and a high degree of overindulgence was de rigueur. But by and large, even there, while I would go beyond Louisa's limit, I did not lose all control. I drove home, for example; not a wise thing, but I did, and sometimes even with Louisa's tacit OK.

Some times, however, the amount I drank would run ahead of me and I would lose control. As I look back on it, I am unable to imagine that I could behave as I did and continue to live a normal-seeming professional and social life. I will recount just a couple of incidents of my going over the top to give you a flavor of what it must have been like for Louisa, never knowing which Bill would emerge in the course of an evening.

I got involved in community theater. There weren't enough people in the "theater going" class to support such normal cultural activities as live theater, so the local English-speaking population had formed a community theater group, which I joined. To give credence to what follows, I must remind you that theatrical lore is replete with stories of the adventures of drunken leading men.

Shortly after I arrived in Guatemala, I was given the part of Henry Drummond in *Inherit the Wind*. It was great fun and it jump-started my Guatemalan thespian career. Before my two years were up, I had been in four plays. Louisa, a great theater lover, supported me to the hilt. She doesn't like to act, though, so at rehearsals I was pretty much on my own. Being at a play rehearsal involves a good bit of just sitting around, especially for actors with small parts. That was my lot when I was King Louis VII of France in *Becket*. I was in many scenes, but never for very long. That's where the small bottles of *indita* came in. I could happily nurse a buzz and still do what was required of me when it was my turn.

Except for one night. I have no recollection of the rehearsal itself that night. No one in the cast chided me the next day for having messed things up or being disruptive, disorderly, or even a little drunk. But still, when we had all said good night and started for home, I found I was not able to find my way. I got around then on a little motor bike, a neat little machine I had bought from my predecessor and which I used to get to and from work. The guerrilla presence in the city at the time had not yet done any violence to Americans. I liked my little low-key motorbike because I argued that no self-respecting guerrilla would ever believe someone on such an insignificant vehicle would be worth kidnapping. After the rehearsal, I set out on it for home in the rain.

Guatemala City, with its numbered *avenidas* crossing at right angles the numbered *calles,* is usually an easy city to navigate. I was disoriented when I left the rehearsal, however, and headed off any which way, confident that I would come across a landmark I recognized. If I didn't, I could figure out where I was by the numbers. But I saw nothing familiar, and when I stopped under a light to plot my course, I realized my problem. I couldn't for the life of me remember my address. *"Quatorce Avenida, quince zero dos."* It comes right to me now, but that night, in the cold rain, it might as well have been in Chinese. We also lived just off the Avenida de Guadeloupe, a large artery out of town. If I could have called that up I would have been OK. But I was at a loss there, too. It was late, dark, raining hard, and I had no idea where I was, except that I was still in a fairly prosperous part of town identified by the high walls that encircled all the houses. These walls were all I could see as I putted around in random circles, getting colder and wetter. Dogs barked as I passed gates, and I could hear the private police, blowing their whistles at appointed times and places to prove they were still awake and making their rounds.

I didn't panic, but did become concerned. For one thing, I was getting really cold and I wanted to go to bed. Surely there must be something I could do. I have said that the houses were surrounded by walls, but many driveways had barred gates you could see through. As I passed one such, I could see not only lights but people inside in a brightly lit, warm, inviting looking living room. I went past but turned and came back. Yes, clearly, warm, dry people, and so close. I made a couple more passes and made up my mind to ask for help. I rang the bell at the gate. I could see someone inside go to their intercom. *"Alo,"* I heard through the speaker, tentatively.

*"Alo,"* I said. "I am Bill Newlin. I work at the American Embassy. I am cold, and wet, and lost, and I need help." I am pretty sure I spoke in English. Maybe his *"alo"* gave him away as an American, or maybe something about the way they all dressed or behaved, or maybe just because English is what I speak. Anyway, he answered in kind. He asked a few questions. He turned into the room full of people and you could tell they were talking back and forth. Then he turned back to the intercom and said, "Wait." He then wrapped himself up in a big coat, got an umbrella, and came out in the rain to open the gate and let a stranger— me—into his house in the middle of the night.

Now, I try to put myself in his shoes. Would I have welcomed this bedraggled, sopping wet, drunken (I was, but did they know it?) man inside to drip all over my tiles? They asked me a million questions, made a couple of phone calls, found my address, and with a minimum of embarrassing questions about how I became so helpless, pointed me off in the right direction. Home I went, uneventfully. I never even learned who my rescuers were. No one ragged me about it in the morning, or ever. Not they, whoever they were, nor the people they had called.

When I got home, I let myself in quietly, stripped off my soaking clothes, left them in the outdoor laundry area where they would be taken by someone—not Louisa—in the morning, dried off quietly in the bathroom, and slipped unnoticed into bed beside my innocent, sleeping wife.

It is said that God watches over drunks and fools. In Guatemala, we were told this job fell to the dog-faced Cadejo, whose image cropped up in paintings and statues. The Crazy House had come with a lovely green one, painted on a wood slab that hung in a hallway. He had certainly been looking out for me that night.

One of the worst parts of drinking too much is its effect on others. Louisa took the brunt of my drinking and was the most deeply hurt by it, but it spilled over to the kids, too. I think it was in Guatemala that the children began to realize their father had a problem. I remember one afternoon I had Nick and Eliza alone. Bill may have been with Louisa. I remember much of that afternoon as a dream. What I remember was driving in a small town, maybe at Lake Amatitlán. I knew I had had too much to drink and I was driving very slowly to avoid trouble, but I managed to scrape a truck anyway as I was getting out of a parking place. The owners of the truck, clearly poor and uneducated *campesinos,* were there, saw it all, and wanted compensation. If only I had had a wad of dollars in my pocket, I would have tried to settle with them on the spot, but I only had two twenties, which would not have done the trick. They had been wronged and wanted redress. What I wanted was to get away from there just as fast as I possibly could. I especially wanted no cops. I proposed, as persuasively as I could, that they go now to establish how much the repairs would cost, and that they come to the embassy on Monday morning, where I would be pleased to give them that sum. I gave them my very official-looking card, with the great seal of the United States of America embossed on it in raised blue ink, which I said they should present to the guard. I would then come to the door and give them the money and make everything right. I was insistent, but it was not my persuasive personality that persuaded them. It was the magic of that beautiful card that carried the day.

That solved a part of the problem for the time being, but there was another problem. I was still drunk and I was seeing double. This was a new sensation for me. For those who have never experienced it, it manifests itself just as it sounds. You see everything twice, the second image next to the first. The problem when you are driving is that it isn't clear which of the images is the one that counts. My solution was to shut one eye, restoring me to the single image state. That, thought I, solved the driving problem.

Nicholas, watching me through the rearview mirror, could see I had one eye shut. As he could see me in the mirror, I could see him. I remember so well his puzzled face and the helplessness I felt, and my fear. It was not our safety I feared for. I believed I would get us all home safely. The drunk always wants to think his driving is unaffected. What I feared was that I would get caught driving drunk with my kids. I stopped at a playground, where I killed some time and sobered up some. I played some one-eye-shut games with them both, especially Nick, to make our peek-a-boo game in the car seem normal. The drive home was uneventful, and I had several hours to sober up before Louisa got home. When she arrived, I said nothing about the scrape and better yet, neither did either kid. It had just been grown-up talk.

On Monday morning, with three hundred dollars in twenties in my pocket, I was sober again and ready for anything. About halfway through the morning a marine guard called to tell me there were some guys speaking Spanish at the front door, flashing my card and asking to speak to me. What should they do? I said I would come right down.

My friends from Sunday had gotten themselves decked out in their best city clothes and by the time I arrived they seemed much reassured by how things were going. I was known at the address on the official card; the soldier in the really snappy blue uniform had listened to them politely;

and then had summoned me. The delegation produced its paper showing how much to fix the dent—eighty something dollars. I gave five twenties and said I didn't want any change. Everything was going to be fine. What had happened the day before was an amusing incident from the past. Perhaps the American had had too much to drink? Couldn't that happen to anyone? We parted the best of friends. The marine guard was a bit mystified, but as he spoke no Spanish, there was lots that happened in Guatemala he didn't understand.

I wondered for years what impact the incident had had on Nick, and a few months ago I asked him. He had no recollection of the afternoon.

Guatemala was a turning point. It was the first time I had been really drunk on the job, and my sneaking drinks at home became much more common blackouts, too, returned to plague me. During bad periods, I couldn't even be counted on to go to a little dinner party of friends and be relied on not to drink too much. Sometimes, when this happened, when my overindulgence would become obvious to others, Louisa would sleep in the guest room. I would awake in the morning to an empty bed and know I was in the doghouse. That could be difficult. I didn't want to admit that I couldn't remember what had happened, but I couldn't very well make a credible apology for the night before without knowing what had transpired.

Sometimes I would wake up with Louisa in the bed with me, but I could not remember how the evening had ended. I would wait on tenterhooks for Louisa to wake up. I wouldn't know if she was going to roll over and say sleepily, "Hi, darling," or if I was going to start the day with "How can you do that to me?"

It was in Guatemala that Louisa began to realize that she—we—had a big problem on our hands. She now tells me that she felt utterly lost. Her tearful pleas to me to quit drinking had no effect, and I tended to get angry when she brought it up. She is a peace-loving person; she feared my anger, and so kept quiet.

## 11

# SKIRTING DANGER ON
# THE GERMAN DESK

FROM GUATEMALA, I WAS ASSIGNED BACK TO WASH-
ington to work at the State Department's German Desk. It
meant moving back into our house on Newark Street and
all the associated comforts of home, but also moving back
into a work situation in the State Department that had led
to serious daytime drinking, which, it could be argued,
had nearly scuttled my Foreign Service career.

In writing about my disastrous Office of Trade Agreements period, and the pulp and paper debacle, I laid much
of the blame on my long and liquid lunch hours. You might
think the shadow of that disaster would have put me on
my guard, but it did not. From the beginning of my tour
in the Office of German Affairs, I continued my practice

of lunching alone whenever I could, and early in the game I moved to a new level of surreptitious drinking from hidden bottles. The structure of the German Desk, however, and my position on it for the first seven months, made any sneaking of drinks difficult. Then my responsibilities on the desk changed and I took over the Berlin brief and also became involved in the negotiation to regularize land access to Berlin, which had been a flash point between the Soviets and the US since the end of WWII.

When I arrived at the German Desk, I was assigned to work very closely with Elwood Williams, "Mr. Germany." I never knew his early history; he may have spent some of his childhood in Germany, but no matter how he had come to it, he had beautiful, fluent German and a deep knowledge of, and respect for, all things German. As Jacques Reinstein and John Auchincloss had in Paris, Williams took me under his wing in Washington. He was going to make a German hand out of me, come what may. From the very beginning, I laid bare my devotion to all things French, and I was not shy about confessing that both Louisa and I had a love affair not only with Paris, but also with nearly every aspect of France and her culture. However, Elwood's confidence in the superiority of things German over things French was so great that he had no doubt he could woo me away from my transitory, and, to his mind, misguided infatuation with France.

One important result of his mission of making a convert of me was that he used my lunch hour as a useful time for my indoctrination. I was used to thinking of that time as my own—the time to get the afternoon buzz started. Elwood saw it as the time to introduce me to a seemingly endless stream of people working in Washington, some in State and others spread around the bureaucracy, who had something useful for me to pick up on the way to fulfilling his ambition of turning me into a Germanophile.

Elwood's, and therefore also my, role in the large Office of German Affairs, was to take care of the myriad day-to-day issues necessary to a smooth relationship between the two countries. We did not have a particular brief—military, economic, or agriculture. Rather, we took care of the usual desk officer duties, handling official visits, telegrams, briefing papers, congressional and diplomatic mail, plus extensive personal contact with the German Embassy in Washington, and with the White House and other agencies of the federal government. We were in charge of nuts and bolts.

In some jobs—my unfortunate experience with pulp and paper is a good case in point—an officer will have one or several projects or papers that take up weeks or even months of his time. Elwood's and my workload was quite different. Every day we would get a sheaf of papers from a nearly infinite variety of sources—the general public, the

German Embassy, our embassy in Bonn, our consulates in Germany, and U.S. embassies and consulates all over the world. We would discuss what needed attention, make a plan of who would do what, and set to work.

One result of this flood of issues that needed attention was that we were in regular contact with a wide variety of people all over the government who had bits of the German pie. Elwood saw that as the perfect way to introduce me to all these people who had been helpful to him in the past and would be so to me if I only knew where to go for help.

Elwood suffered from advanced multiple sclerosis. He worked from a wheelchair, assisted by a nurse who took his dictation, turned his pages as he read, fed him, helped him smoke, and helped him in the bathroom. I often thought it was, at least in part, his realization that his period as Germany's advocate in U.S. halls of power was coming to an end that prompted him to work as hard and as fast as he could to groom a successor. Whatever the reason, my speedy education was his highest priority. So there went most of my lunch hours. Mind you, I enjoyed most of those entertaining and informative sessions and I met many interesting people—but at the cost of going without alcohol.

If I couldn't count on drinking at lunch, I had to make other arrangements. I was at the point that alcohol had become essential to my daily routine. I fell back on the system that had served me in Guatemala. There, I bought and sequestered little bottles of *indita*. The equivalent in Washington was half pints of vodka. These fit nearly as handily as the *indita* bottles into a pants pocket without a bulge, and were easy to hide either inside the building or out. I became like a squirrel, with my little bottles stashed away close to hand—but unlike a squirrel, I never forgot where I hid my stash.

The car was the best place. I always had a bottle under the rubber mat on the driver's side, up under the seat. It was easy to extract and to replace, even while driving. Its presence at that time allowed me to take a big slide in the wrong direction, because it became my practice to have a slug on the way to work. That made up for being unable to count on lunchtime. But every smart rabbit has three holes; I was not limited to my car.

One of my favorite spots was in an alley right across from the State Department headquarters. A window air conditioner jutted into the alley, and there was just room for a half-pint bottle to slip up under the unit onto the sill. It was invisible, yet easy to retrieve and replace. That was perfect until one day, when I reached confidently for my hidden treasure, only to find a void. Some scoundrel had discovered my hidey-hole and beaten me to it. I continued to use that spot, and more often than not, my bottle was untouched, but from time to time the phantom boozer had beaten me to the punch. I deeply resented him.

Another good spot was under an overpass right in front of a side entrance to our building. Right after that overpass had been constructed, I enjoyed nearly six months of free parking in a little pull-off underneath it, where the cops seemed not to notice my little blue Fiat. Once they were onto me, however, they ticketed me every day and I had to cease and desist. That spot no longer served as a parking place, but it was easily reached on foot and a small pile of large rocks that had been left behind served well as a place to stash a small bottle. The only problem was that once I no longer had a car parked there, I would have been hard put to explain what I was doing walking in plain sight from the Department, across the service road, and down a steep, grassy hill, only to disappear under the overpass, then, in five or so minutes, to casually repeat the route in reverse. Happily, if anyone ever noticed me, they had the discretion to let well enough alone.

On days when I could lunch alone—and in spite of Elwood's education efforts there were some—I would enjoy my customary two or three one-and-a-half-ounce mini bottles of bourbon. On Elwood lunch days, I would typically visit one of my bottles once in the late morning, again in mid-afternoon and finally in the late afternoon. And of course, I would take a pull from the bottle under the seat on the ride to work in the morning and on the ride home at night.

All these bottles had to be periodically replaced, of course—a half pint is only eight ounces, or about five or six good swigs. To restock, I would avail myself of one of three liquor stores in the area. I used three, because I didn't want any single one to realize how many of the little things I consumed in a week. Even with my custom spread around to three stores, any one of them would have been able to identify the guy who at least once a week came in his pinstripe suit and bought a telltale half pint. Who but an alcoholic would regularly buy those little bottles? Of course, that is what I was.

I am unable to reconstruct now how I reacted to my rather steady descent into alcoholism. I take as a given that the little alcoholic edge I carried with me and nurtured throughout the day detracted from my effectiveness. I know that to be so, but every once in a while, boozing gave me a lift. Here is an example of a time when my morning pull in the car on the drive in may have given me the courage to take a risk—one that paid off.

A regular occurrence was being visited by high-level officials, and one such visit was from Willy Brandt, who came to Washington when he was the German foreign minister during the NATO ministers meeting that celebrated its 20th anniversary. The NATO presidency rotates among the members, and it was Germany's turn in the chair, so Willy Brandt was president. Each foreign minister had a control officer to ensure everything went smoothly, and I was Willy Brandt's. It was my job to stick to him like a burr and make sure he did what he was supposed to when he was supposed to do it. This meant, among other things, riding in the car with him at all times.

The very first morning began with a motorcade of some twenty stretch limousines all flying their national flags. Willy and I, in the German limo, led the pack. It was impressive. We pulled up to the building where the first plenary session was to be held. The ministers—with their control officers—filed ceremoniously into the building. There was plenty of time for the limos to circle around the block and line up at the entrance in exactly the same order they had arrived. Easy.

Except that when Brandt and I exited the building, expecting to find the German Mercedes first in line for the ride to the State Department, there was no German car to be seen. The first car in line flew the Turkish flag, then came the French, then the Greeks. We could see all the way to the corner—about a dozen cars. No German flag anywhere. In fact, there seemed to be no rhyme or reason to their order. What to do? And who in the world was to make that decision? Fortunately, I had taken an extra large swig from my bottle on the way to work only an hour before. I was primed for the occasion. I took Brandt firmly by the elbow and led him to the first car in line—the Turkish car, flying their colors. The snappy-looking chauffeur gave the car a little touch of throttle to indicate his eagerness to proceed. I opened the passenger door and helped (pushed?) Willy Brandt in.

"Is this the right thing to do?" he asked, rather tentatively, decidedly uncomfortable in the foreign car.

"Absolutely, Mr. Foreign Minister," I said as I shut the door, sealing him in, and scurried around and got in the other side. "Go to the Diplomatic entrance of the State Department." The driver didn't even turn around. He had his orders. He slid his big car into the roadway and toward our destination. As we pulled off, I was glad to see that the rest of the ministers were just getting into the next car in line with no thought to nationality. We arrived at the State Department with the cars all jumbled, but the ministers in perfect protocol order. The rest of the morning was uneventful.

Later in the day, during a break, a man I recognized as the protocol officer in charge of the meeting, who had briefed the control officers a few days before, came up to me purposefully.

"Are you the guy who put Brandt in the Turkish car and drove off?" he asked.

"I am he," I admitted.

He took my hand in both of his, looked me right in the eye, and squeezed. "Oh, Jesus, thank you," he said. "You should have a medal." He turned on his heel and disappeared. Without that extra swig in my little Fiat, we might be there still.

The piece I find hard to fit into this puzzle is how I could possibly have had such a complicated drinking regime and not been immediately found out. My secret must have laid in the fact that I managed to keep just under the threshold of obvious drinking behavior. On the other hand, I was well over the level that would have allowed me to function at my best. I did what was required of me at my work, but I did not take the initiatives that would have been expected of me—that I would have expected of myself, had I not shackled my own hands.

As with Reinstein, I always wondered what in the world Elwood was thinking. He must have known I was drinking; yet he never gave me an inkling that he disapproved of the way I was behaving.

Looking back, I feel a deep shame over my time at the German Desk—more than I feel about other wasted opportunities. Elwood liked me and did everything he could to cultivate in me the same affinity for the German people as he had. He continued to introduce me to interesting people both at the center and the fringes of the U.S./German world. He arranged for me to take trips to Germany, one to visit all the Consulates General, and another to Berlin. He did his best for me, but I never gave him my best.

My work with Elwood dealing with the basic German Desk issues had lasted a little under a year when I was assigned to work on Berlin affairs. This assignment consisted of two quite separate types of work. I was essentially the Berlin Desk officer, which gave me responsibility for all matters connected to our continued occupation role in West Berlin. These were similar to a range of issues I had covered with Elwood but also included the problems related to access to Berlin. In this category fell maintaining the elaborate contingency plans surrounding access to Berlin. Some other quite unique Berlin-related issues included the continued incarceration of Rudolf Hess at Spandau Prison and the management of the Berlin Document Center, the allied repository of Nazi records.

My work on Berlin affairs was an especially interesting assignment. Berlin was, at that time, still one of the potential flash points in the Cold War. To simplify greatly, at war's end, Germany was divided into an eastern sector under Soviet control and a western sector controlled by the four Quadripartite powers: the US, the UK, France, and Russia. Berlin was an enclave in the middle of the Soviet sector. What made this such a sensitive and dangerous problem was that through some careless drafting, the post-war agreements gave the Western Powers guaranteed access from Berlin across East Germany to the west only by air. The agreement was silent about passage by land or water. The Soviets, of course, took silence to mean they retained all but air rights.

In June 1948, the Soviets, in an effort to put pressure on the allies, exercised what they claimed as their right and blockaded all land and water access to Berlin. General Eisenhower organized the Berlin Airlift and for a year Berlin was supplied by allied aircraft, mostly U.S. but augmented by British, French, Canadian, and others. They flew over 200,000 flights. By the spring of 1949, the airlift was carrying more cargo than had been entering Berlin from all sources at the beginning of the crisis. Faced by the great success of the airlift, the Soviets backed down and ended their land and water blockade. Access to Berlin—for a time—was open.

Nevertheless, Berlin continued to be a danger point, as the Soviets periodically tested the Western resolve by temporarily closing down the non-air access to Berlin. This was the backdrop for one of the best-known speeches of the Cold War. In June 1963, John F. Kennedy, visiting Berlin, delivered a speech in which he used the German phrase, *"Ich bin ein Berliner!"* ("I am a Berliner!") to underline the continued Western resolve to stand with West Berliners in the face of their understandable fear of annexation by the Soviets. The Kennedy resolve notwithstanding, the

Soviets continued to test the Allies with periodic blockades; the possibility of the use of force by one side or the other was a real danger.

My period on the German Desk coincided with negotiations to regularize the Berlin situation. It was, of course, complicated by the fact that any agreement would first have to satisfy the Washington agencies with a stake in the solution—notably Defense and the National Security Council, but also many more on the fringes, like Commerce and Treasury. Then our allies would have to adapt a unified position, and the West as a whole needed to satisfy the Soviets. This all finally came together and in June 1972, the agreement was signed by the Western powers and the Soviet Union. In the agreement, all parties agreed that disputes about Berlin would be settled by peaceful measures. The central provision was that the Soviets agreed that all land and water access to West Berlin would be both unimpeded and facilitated. This agreement finally removed from the table one of the last potential areas of conflict remaining from the post-war settlement.

Until then, the risk was not just theoretical; it was real. An elaborate set of contingency plans had been developed, dealing with the various anticipated Soviet initiatives. These plans were regularly dusted off and tested in exercises simulating Soviet challenges and the allied responses.

Surprisingly, I thought, I was given a central role in the U.S. planning for, participation in, and critique of these exercises. Regarding the critique, which took place in Brussels, I was sent as Washington's sole representative.

During this period in which I was given considerable latitude to act independently, I was still drinking regularly on the job. The little bottle still lived under the seat of the car, and it was a part of my morning and evening commute. I still had lunch alone as often as I could, counting on the opportunity to drink at least two, most likely more, little bottles of bourbon. My drinking during this period continued to be excessive, but I was reined in by the level of responsibility I had been given.

I was certainly not, however, out of the woods. The critique of the exercise in Brussels nearly did me in. I had added on to that Brussels visit a stop in Berlin. I was looking forward to taking the train out of Berlin, through the German Democratic Republic (GDR) to the West. I was also counting on the time on the train to pull together my notes for the presentation that I was scheduled to give the next day. Putting off my writing assignments until the very last minute was part of my modus operandi. In this case I had more than simple procrastination working against me. The whole train experience was too much out of a Le Carré novel to allow work to be even remotely possible for me. How could preparing a talk about a boring exercise to protect the free world compete with the real-life drama of a train trip behind the Iron Curtain?

I was the only official passenger on the train, and I had a compartment in a car that seemed to be empty but for me; but that didn't mean they didn't serve a good dinner. I partook and washed it all down with three of those little bottles of good wine they used to have on European trains. I had a nice white Burgundy with the sole, a red Bordeaux for the meat, and another red because the first one ran out and there was still cheese. Not surprisingly, I slept soundly, disturbed only by periodic paper controls by stern but polite officials.

The embassy took good care of me, gave me a good place to shower and shave, and delivered me to the appointed place in plenty of time. Mine was the key talk, summarizing what we had done and what we had learned. This speech had been on the schedule for weeks—months. Regularly, I had blocked out time to write it up. But now, on the morning of the presentation, I had no prepared text.

The morning could have gone two ways. I could have blown it. Easily. Not only did I not have a speech written out, but I didn't even really have good notes. What I had written on a yellow pad on the train the night before was useless. What I did have were topic headings I had jotted on the back of an envelope in the car on the way to the conference.

As it turned out, I aced the presentation. True, I had never written out my talk, but I had gone over it enough in my head that, quite miraculously, I found I had no trouble retrieving it and laying it out clearly. I didn't even need my envelope. With the major headings straight, the rest seemed easy. There was one tricky place in the exercise and the appropriate U.S. response was counterintuitive. One of the Brits tried to correct me on a minor point dealing with this area. But it was he who had it backwards and who had to back down and shamefacedly admit his error once I patiently straightened him out. The question period was actually fun.

At the end of the day, one of the secretariat people came up to me and asked if I could give them a copy of my talk for their record. I allowed as how I would like to oblige but as perhaps he had noticed, I had not read from a paper as most of the participants had. Surely, said my interlocutor, I had a speech somewhere that I had memorized. "No," I said, "just this envelope," which I gave him.

The rest of the critique went well. This time my Cadejo looked after me. When I got back to Washington, my boss called me in to pass on praise he had gotten about my performance from senior U.S. naval officers and the foreign delegates. "A job well done, Newlin," he said, and I thanked him.

**12**

# PLAYING LOOSE WITH NATIONAL SECURITY

THERE IS A PART OF THE STATE DEPARTMENT THAT never sleeps. When something serious happens on the other side of the globe in the middle of the night, the Operation Center, which is staffed in three eight-hour shifts so it can be open 24/7/365, is where the problem gets dumped. Each shift is headed by a senior watch officer, whose official title is deputy director of operations, or DDO. My next posting was as a DDO of the Operation Center.

The job was officially described as follows: "The DDO is the Department's principal duty officer. He is responsible to the executive secretary of the Department for assistance in handling the Department's urgent business, particularly outside regular hours. He must be prepared to alert and brief senior Department officials, including the Secretary, about significant developments, and to coordinate U.S. government actions with the White House, CIA, and other offices dealing with foreign affairs."

During regular hours, an important DDO function is to coordinate activities of special task forces formed to develop policy and to carry out operations involving major problem situations. If the crisis were to become long lived—like the Iran Hostage crisis, for example—a task force would be organized and the Op Center would be relieved of its crisis management function. But often, in the case of the many short-lived crises, the Op Center, and therefore the DDO, would become the point person for days, or even weeks, on end.

Still, it is after hours that the DDO really comes into his own. It is he or she who must decide how to respond to the many messages that arrive when the Department's offices are closed—what, if anything needs to be done and who must be alerted. Most of the time the alerting function is fairly routine. There is a State Department duty officer system in place after hours for every substantive bureau. For example, the Bureau of European Affairs has a duty officer to whom issues relating to Europe would be referred. It wasn't rocket science deciding into which duty officer's lap to drop most problems. One problem arose because most of the issues involved classified information, which couldn't be discussed over the telephone. A certain amount of doublespeak went on, trying to help the bureau duty officer decide if she could go back to sleep or if she would have to come to the Department to read the telegram in question before deciding what to do about the problem.

The situation was further complicated by the U.S. government's security system. Many people on the outside think Top Secret is the top security category. In fact, the classification regime is more complicated than that and is based on the principle of "need to know." The theory is that even if you are cleared for top secret, your access to any classified messages is guided by your need to know. When dealing with particularly sensitive issues, distribution limitations are superimposed on top of the security ones. Messages were marked either Limited Distribution (Limdis), Executive Distribution (Exdis), or (I am not making this up) No Distribution (Nodis). (The details may have changed since my time, but not the principle.) The Nodis category was reserved for only the most sensitive messages and at night, the distribution of Nodis messages was handled in the code room by only the senior officer on duty, sealed by him, and hand carried to the Op Center to be delivered to the hands of the DDO who decided what, if any, further action or wider or narrower distribution was required.

State Department bureau duty officers were not cleared to see Nodis messages, and any communication about Nodis telegrams had to be conducted at the Assistant Secretary level, at least. Many Nodis telegrams were sensitive but not urgent, and could therefore wait for opening of business for distribution. On the other hand, many were time sensitive and DDOs would regularly wake the very senior officers in the middle of the night for guidance. (A footnote to history was that Henry Kissinger, when he was secretary of state, was averse to talking on the secure phone that linked his residence and the Op Center, often preferring to use a regular phone line, which had better reception. Some highly sensitive issues were briefed in plain language.)

I describe the functions of the Op Center in some detail in hopes of giving you an idea of both the sensitive nature of the job, and its complexities. There were, of course, nights where precious little of note happened in the world and the DDO had an easy ride. But it could be a wild ride, too. A contemporary internal description of the Operation Center's activities reads: "The Operation Center (can be) a veritable beehive of activity; to an outsider, it would look like bedlam. All the phones are often in use and others are ringing. The senior man, the DDO, is the person who must bring order out of this apparent chaos."

It was not the job for an officer who regularly slipped down to the basement garage for a big swig of vodka from the bottle under the front seat of the car. But that was how I handled it.

I won't dwell on the day shift, 8:00 a.m. to 4:00 p.m. or the 4:00 p.m. to midnight shifts. Both of them were relatively unstressful and routine. It is not surprising that my regular nipping wasn't a major problem. But the midnight to 8:00 a.m. shift could be challenging and demanding, and in retrospect I find it quite remarkable that no one ever called me out for drinking on the job.

My drinking routine in those days began on the drive to work, when I would take a big, three-ounce glug from my under-the-seat bottle. The oncoming DDO would report an hour early to overlap with, and obtain a briefing from, his outgoing counterpart. My practice was, after this briefing, and ten minutes before taking over the watch, to slip down to the garage for a final pre-shift pick-me-up. I would repeat that trip at least twice more (usually three times) in the course of the watch, each time for a two- or three-ounce slug. You might wonder about the smell of my breath. Early on, I restricted my drinking to vodka to avoid detection. But I soon discovered it didn't matter what I drank. No one seemed to notice anything suspicious on my breath. So at least for my lunchtime libation, I moved back to my drink of choice—bourbon.

I am reminded of the story apocryphally told of Churchill's personal secretary, who, after the great man's death was asked if the rumors of Churchill's constant drinking were true. The aide was delighted, he said, to put that old canard to rest. In doing so, he ticked off a remarkable succession of ritual drinks imbibed by Churchill during a typical day, starting before breakfast and ending with the last nightcap. The secret, it turned out, was the spacing: At no time did Churchill have any more than a little buzz on. That was my way. My little visits to the garage only resulted in a few ounces each visit, for a total of six to ten ounces. Spread that out over a ten-hour shift and it isn't much more than a somewhat hard-drinking social drinker would have at a long dinner.

Of course, I would go over the limit from time to time. That was more apt to happen in social settings or at home, but it could also happen at work. On one particularly egregious episode, I started off to work at about 10:30 p.m. after a more than usually liquid dinner. I did not compensate by cutting down on my commute libations, so my blood alcohol level was above normal when I started my shift, and it never came down. It was a busy watch, but not unmanageable, and I felt I was pretty well on top of things, until near the end, when things got away from me.

One important function of the outgoing DDO after the midnight to 8:00 a.m. shift is to prepare a daily log, which would form the basis of a report to key officials both in and out of the State Department of the important events of the previous night. At the end of the midnight shift, at about eight in the morning, the DDO would go to the Secretary's office, give the Executive Secretary the log, and brief him on it.

The running log is maintained by the DDO with the assistance of an editor. My practice was to make log entries as we went along, jotting handwritten notes, with the time and the action to be noted, to my editor. He would tidy up the language and keep a running, typed log that would form the backbone of my briefing. On especially busy nights, it sometimes happened I would get behind on making log entries and the editor would help out. On the night in question, largely due to my higher-than-usual alcohol blood level, I was way behind on my log notes. Then, near the end of the watch, a crisis developed that took all my attention, so I not only failed to give my editor the relatively routine notes from early in the watch, but I did not give him notes on the crisis either.

I watched the clock move inexorably toward the witching hour, 7:30, when I would have to go, log in hand, to brief the Executive Secretary. But I knew my last log entry had been hours before. The time came. Ready or not, I had to go upstairs and face the music. I gathered my inadequate notes and was pulling my thoughts together in my head, when my editor handed me a lovely three-page log that brought us right up to date.

"You'll need this," he said.

"Right, thanks," I said, and up I went.

I had a few minutes in the elevator and in the outer office before the briefing started, so I had time to review my editor's excellent notes. The briefing went fine, and when I came back to the Op Center, I had a chance for a little more in the way of a "thank you."

"I really appreciated that," I said.

"Glad to do it," said he.

That was it. No mention of alcohol—then, or ever. But of course he knew, and he saved my bacon.

I have just reread my performance ratings from my Op Center tour. Nowhere in them is there any suggestion that I was not up to the task or was operating under any disadvantage of any kind. In fact, they were gratifyingly positive. But functioning in the office is only half the story. At home, I was heading for a bad fall.

# 13

## THE FINCA

WHEN WE LIVED IN GUATEMALA, OUR CHILDREN suffered various deprivations compared to their Guatemalan friends. First Communion (or the lack of it) ranked high on the list, because it brought the celebrant lots of presents. Not having cousins was another lacuna, one that our middle son Nicholas overcame by announcing that he and his best friend Joseph were cousins. But there was nothing he or we could do to make up for the fact that everyone but us—and the other unfortunate Americans—seemed to have a *finca*—farm—to which they repaired on weekends and holidays. In some cases, these were vast establishments on whose sugar fields or coffee trees the family fortune was based. Other *fincas* were just weekend escapes. But one way or another, it seemed that most Guatemalans we knew (private-school

Guatemalans, to be sure) could and did retreat to the *finca* on weekends, leaving the deprived Americans cadging for an invitation.

When we got home to Washington, one of the things we wanted to find was our own weekend place. Country establishments, owned and run by grandparents, had been a staple part of growing up for both Louisa and me, with regular weekends in the country. We wanted the same for our kids. As there were no grandparents in the Washington picture, we had to find a place of our own.

We had a lot of fun looking, and in the fall of 1970, we found the perfect spot. It was in Maryland's Catoctin Mountains, only an hour and a quarter from Washington. The house sat at the end of a long lane, well back from the road. It was stone on the first floor and log on the second. A large land bank barn was set into the side of the hill, and a summer kitchen had been converted into a guest bedroom. The summer kitchen's most distinctive characteristics were its huge fireplace, with a spit that swung out for serious, nineteenth-century cooking, and an incongruous school bell, with its own cupola, that the children never tired of ringing. The headwaters of Hunting Creek—which offered good trout fishing downstream—ran right by the compound, and there was a farm pond full of sunnies and big bass. Right outside the front door, under a grape arbor laden with Concord grapes in summer, was a pump that really pumped water. The whole place was right out of a storybook.

We finally had our own weekend farm, so of course we named it "The Finca." In the early years, we went out there most weekends. The kids loved playing in the barn, climbing, and swinging on the swings. In the stream, they caught crayfish and made dams to create pools. The pond provided hours of fishing pleasure. It was always fun to catch sunnies, but there was more serious business, too. The right-sized sunny was the perfect bait for the big bass. Nick caught one that weighed in at over five pounds on the butcher's scale in the local market.

Winter brought its own entertainment. Back then, winters were cold enough to freeze the pond for skating, which became a favorite pastime. If snow covered the ice, the snow itself became the preferred medium. Snowmen, snowball fights, and forts occupied us all until the kids got old enough to ski a half-hour away at Charnita, which later morphed into Ski Liberty.

What's wrong with this picture? Over the years, my drinking began, little by little, to poison The Finca. My downfall there was secret drinking. That's not to say I wouldn't sometimes overdo it just by having too many drinks right in front of everybody. Instead of the one and a dividend that I was allowed—by custom—to have, I would have three, or even four, and then it would be obvious that

I was no longer myself. Louisa hated when that happened, but she wanted to keep the peace, so she tried not to make too much of it.

My secret drinking at The Finca was more destructive. The biggest threat was when I would go out there by myself. Louisa was the person who didn't like me to drink. Therefore, when I was away from her, especially alone, I persuaded myself that nobody cared if I drank, or how much. So long as I could time my drinking so that on returning, I could not be seen to have outrageously overindulged, I was home free. So I would plan little trips to The Finca alone. Sometimes there would be something that needed to be done. Especially at the beginning, but throughout our tenure there, little things always needed attention. Even a house as small as The Finca had all the moving parts a larger one has. There was plenty for me to do on any weekend. Sometimes, I would just precede the others by a few hours—or come home a little later. However I did it, I could carve out a few hours in which I could have a bit too much to drink in peace.

The other kind of secret drinking was perhaps even more insidious. A farm is a big place. Think of all the places a guy could hide a little vodka bottle on a farm! The barn was a natural. The lower part of the barn, where it was cut into the hill, was not favored by the kids. The upper part was light, and had the swings and ladders to climb and bales of hay for forts. The lower part was pretty dark, dank even in daytime, and spidery; it was easy for me to slip a little bottle in a high nook, where two logs didn't fit together very well. Only I could even reach that high, let alone have the nerve to poke a hand into that dark hole. So if I wanted a midmorning swig to put a little edge on my mood, I had only to slip out to the barn on some pretext. Or up to the end of the pond where a hollow log provided the necessary hiding place; or out to the end of the lane, in a crevice between the rocks that held up one of the posts supporting a sign that read "The Finca."

One of the most pernicious aspects of secret drinking is the deceitfulness it engenders. Here we were, a little family in an idyllic setting, pursuing innocent pleasures right out of a *Saturday Evening Post* cover by Norman Rockwell, and in the midst of it all, me sneaking out from time to time to take a little nip from one of my sequestered bottles.

It took a while for the fact to register that The Finca was not just a place that brought out the drinking side of me, but a place where drinking would sometimes get the better of me. But in time, that reality became apparent, and Louisa and I began to view it from different perspectives. I saw it in a positive light, as a place where I had a better chance of drinking a little too much and getting away with it, and Louisa began to fear it as a place where I was more at risk of overindulging than at home.

I have perhaps made my drinking at The Finca seem like an innocent game, with me fooling the rest of the family by slipping off from time to time to take a tiny swallow from one of the little bottles I had so cleverly stashed away, unbeknownst to anyone. In truth, however, one terrible fact about my drinking was that I could keep it in bounds only some of the time, and I never knew when it would get out of hand. I must now recount one such time which led to the darkest moment of my life, when I simply could not see how I could go on with life at all.

Louisa, twelve-year-old Nick, ten-year-old Eliza, and I had spent the weekend at The Finca. Billy was home on vacation from his first year at St. Paul's. We probably came in two cars, as Louisa must have had something in Washington that drew her home early on Sunday afternoon. Billy went with her. I was to follow with the other two kids. But I got drunk. Not just drunk in my subtle, hard-to-spot fog, but stumbling, falling-down drunk.

Many of the details of that afternoon have entirely escaped me. I recently asked Nick, who is now in his fifties, to recount his recollection of that afternoon to me. He says that at one point I began to act somewhat weirdly, but he didn't make too much of it. Then he caught me in the kitchen taking a big swig from a bottle, and he confronted me. I denied any problem, but he was upset. He became really worried when I showed up, after a brief disappearance, with burdock burrs all over my clothes and even in my hair. I must have gone through, or even fallen down in, a big burdock patch on my way to or from a bottle stashed in a field somewhere. "It was," he says now, nearly forty years later, "quite a visual."

Eliza was frightened by seeing her father clearly out of control and looking like a huge, dirty animal (my characterization). She retreated to her upstairs bedroom. Nick had the good sense to get my keys and join his sister. Not much later, he was surprised when he heard the car start and saw it disappear down the lane. He had confiscated the house keys by mistake.

Nick called home and explained to Louisa what had happened, and she came and got him and Eliza. She found them still huddled in the locked upstairs bedroom. She took them home, calmed them down, and put them to bed. She then had what must have been the worst night of her life. She was focusing not so much on the fact that her husband had gotten drunk and abandoned her children, as on the fact that, because he was driving around dead drunk, she might no longer have a husband at all.

Evidently after leaving The Finca, I drove around aimlessly. I was sober enough to drive and to realize what I had done—realized my act had been so reprehensible that I could never go back and face Louisa and the children. What I had already done—driving off and leaving my

ten- and twelve-year-old children to fend for themselves—
was so unimaginable that I couldn't possibly imagine going
on with life anyway. It got dark, and I pulled off the road
to try to figure out if there were, could be, any acceptable
next steps. I couldn't see any. I began to drive again, and
came upon a motel. It was late by then, and I was tired, so I
stopped and got a room.

Lying awake, fully clothed on the bed, it became clear
there was only one possible course of action. My life was
over. My children, whom I treasured above all else, had
been betrayed by me. The notion that my actions had
caused them fear or danger was unthinkable to me. I would
never be able to face either my wife or my children—nor
any friends, once the shabby story got out, which of course
it would—so I had to end my life. How? At home, I had
a shotgun and some shells. Although I had sometimes
toyed with the idea of suicide when feeling overwhelmed
by work back in my days at Harvard Business School, that
had just been a mental game. This was for real—this time,
there was really no other way out, or so I thought, lying
there on the motel bed. But I couldn't go home to get the
gun. The other obvious method was to simply crash into
an oncoming truck. But I couldn't bear the thought that I
might take another life—another father's, perhaps.

Maybe I didn't need to kill myself after all. Perhaps
I could just go into hiding. Lying on top of the spread in

the dingy motel room, I tried to figure out how I could get what I would need to disappear. I would need money. Could I get to my broker in Washington before the hue and cry reached him, before he realized I was a wanted man? How quickly could I get him to give me a hundred thousand dollars in cash to bankroll my escape? I would need to leave the country. Go south to Central America. Surely a gringo could hole up in some mountain village and not be found? I invented a life for myself, eating beans and tortillas, working in the fields with the *campesinos,* early to bed, early to rise, teaching the villagers' children English. But none of that would work. I would need a passport, and my car would be traced. I would be caught and brought home. The simple fact was that I could not envision any viable life available to me. I was still under forty, and my life seemed over.

I slipped in and out between waking, deep sleep, and dreaming. Morning came, and I no longer had the luxury of being able to escape into a half-dream world. I was fully awake. Everything was true; the worst had happened. Drunk, I had left my children alone at The Finca. Where were they now? How were they? I couldn't call Louisa. I could never talk to Louisa again. How could I possibly face even her voice? But how could I not check up on the kids?

In the daylight, I couldn't kill myself. I couldn't run away. My options had narrowed and then disappeared. All

I could do was go home and face everybody. I couldn't—but worse, I couldn't not. I called Louisa. Her focus was on my still being alive rather than on my behavior. Yes, I still had a home.

To my great relief, and even more to my surprise, Louisa and the kids appeared more happy to see me home alive, than angry over what I had done. But I couldn't escape my actions. I had to live with the shame.

We couldn't pretend nothing had happened. Louisa had by now begun seeing a therapist—as I thought of him, a "shrink." There had been tears, there had been pleading, and she was already seeing how my alcohol was affecting her and our life. Characteristically, she blamed herself. Louisa has always had a problem with guilt. The therapist was trying to get her to see that she was not at fault. He recommended that I be hospitalized. Of course, I would not even consider it. I refused to be committed. What to do? A shrink for me, of course. Plus Alcoholics Anonymous, and family therapy. But like the hospital, that was a bridge I couldn't cross. I couldn't go off with my children to talk to a stranger about the day Daddy had gotten drunk and walked out on them. So the family therapy went on for them but without me, with the shrink explaining to the others that I was really there, just not physically.

It's hard to believe that incident did not cure me of my addiction then and there. Hard to believe, having seen where drink could lead me, that I could ever consider taking another drink, but the terrible fact was that I still couldn't imagine a life without alcohol. I went to AA. I pledged never again; I vowed to give it up "one day at a time," but I never really meant it. What I was praying for was not that I would never drink, not even that I would never drink too much. What I longed for was a daily life in which I could go on drinking but always remain in control. A life in which my consumption would stay at a level where only I knew I was drinking. Then, in this fantasy life, from time to time Louisa would go on a trip, or I would, and I would have some time to myself—some time alone when I could just get a nice quiet buzz on and no one would be the wiser.

## 14

# POST-FINCA—BACK
# FROM THE ABYSS

THOUGH THE INCIDENT AT THE FINCA DIDN'T CURE me, it certainly changed my universe. Nothing could, or did, return to what had been normal, or seemingly normal to that point. My drinking and its consequences were now open secrets, at least to the near and dear. I never did go to the family therapy sessions—they went on without me—but I did have to get my own shrink. The shrink doing the family therapy was a wonderful, warm, and intelligent man. He might have been able to help me if I had only let him. But while I could have seen him in the family context— that I was rejecting—he would not take me as a patient all by myself. Instead, I was shunted off to a man who struck me as a cold fish. No rapport developed between us and I fear never could have. As it became clear that the sessions with him were not helping, the psychiatric approach to my attempts at sobriety was allowed to wither away.

I did go to AA. I had gone to a few meetings before the Finca disaster, but now AA was mandatory. I would go every Tuesday night to the Chevy Chase AA meeting in the basement of the Chevy Chase Baptist Church on Western Avenue, just off Chevy Chase Circle.

Actually, my AA experience was very interesting, and in the long run may have been helpful. That particular AA group was pretty upscale. It was a bunch of nondescript people drawn from all along the middle-class spectrum. What brought us together was that we were all in the thrall of something we couldn't shake alone.

A few people were in an emeritus status. They were alcoholics, but secure in their non-drinking condition. Some in that category came to reinforce their own non-drinking resolve. Coming to AA meetings helped them feel solid in their sobriety. Others felt no need of AA for themselves—they had been sober for thirty years. They came for the help they were able to give others still struggling in the grip of the addiction.

The meetings all followed the same pattern. Someone who had been designated to lead off would open the meeting by describing where he was in his alcoholic journey. I say "his," but I would say a good third of the group were women. After five or ten minutes, the lead-off speaker would turn the meeting over to the group and we would go around the room. At the very least, everyone would get as far as "Hi, I'm Bill. I'm an alcoholic." Then you could say that you'd rather just listen, or you could tell your tale.

My maiden voyage went something like this. "Hi, I'm Bill. I'm an alcoholic. I've been drinking too much, on and off, since I was a kid, but a couple of nights ago I got drunk and walked out on my kids. If I don't stop, I'll ruin my life completely, if I haven't already." Then, I laid out a bit of what had happened. When I had finished, there was an undercurrent of people all murmuring, like what I imagined as the "Amens" and the "You tell it, brothers" in response to a sermon at an African-American church. In AA, the responses are different. In AA, it's "Glad you are here" and "You're in the right place."

The meetings are like soap operas. The participants come week after week and each time we get a new chapter of their saga. We all know that Mary had been sober for nearly two years, but that she had slipped badly when her husband left her. She was then back on the straight and narrow. When she said she'd just passed the one-month mark, we clapped. Next was Alice with a different story. We sympathized as she explained that she couldn't get to the one-month mark, no matter how hard she tried; at around three weeks, the sherry bottle in her kitchen just called out to her too loudly, and at about six in the evening. she couldn't get through the preparation of dinner without yielding to that call. We encouraged Alice, and some participants offered hints to help her get over the hump.

It didn't take me long to feel that I belonged here. I filled in the details about my own soap opera. I spoke about the little bottles hidden around my office, and how they pulled at me. I described what happened every time I walked past the liquor closet at home. People listened. Some of them had been right there. Others had had different experiences. I got encouragement and advice. All the stories—or nearly all—were of some interest. It didn't take a great storyteller to make them so. I began to realize that for many, the AA meeting was a big part of their lives. Some of them had been coming for years. AA was their club.

The "dean" of the Chevy Chase AA meeting was a white-haired guy named Fred, who sat up front on the left, which meant he was always the last to speak. "Hi, I'm Fred. I'm an alcoholic." Fred had been sober for more than thirty years. He was one of those who came to help others find the relief that he himself had found. Fred would talk of times years ago when he was drinking and had done something harmful to himself or someone else. Or he would talk of someone once trying to quit, who had been helped over a bad patch by someone else. He was a pretty good raconteur, and often he would pick up on a story someone had just told, and tie a tale to that. "Jack's account of his experience with the bus driver reminds me of a time...," and he would be off.

An entertaining sidelight of the Chevy Chase AA was that you never knew whom you might bump into. No one I knew was a regular, but over the months I attended, several times casual friends and neighbors showed up. Usually, our mutual greeting was as natural as if it were taking place in the supermarket. Only once did I find a meeting awkward. I found myself face to face with a woman of my years whom Louisa and I knew from our proper Philadelphia days and whom we still saw, usually at rather straitlaced affairs. Unlike me, she was clearly flustered by being "caught" at AA, and went to some lengths to assure me she didn't need it, and just came to see what it was like. She never came back, and when we met afterwards, neither of us alluded to it.

A supportive atmosphere of camaraderie prevailed at AA meetings. At the end of all meetings we all joined hands and recited the Serenity Prayer:

> *God grant me the serenity to accept the things*
> *I cannot change,*
> *The courage to change the things I can,*
> *And the wisdom to know the difference.*

Everyone would then squeezes the hand of the person on either side of them and say: "Keep coming back." And I did.

But coming back didn't cure me. Every day I didn't have a drink was a singular triumph that cost me dearly. AA's proponents say of its program that you stop one day at a time, and they are right. An alcoholic can consider staying sober for the next twenty-four hours, but the idea of being sober for a year, or even a month, or even just a week is too much of a commitment. When a dry day is over, a day in which you didn't drink so much as a tiny drop, you have gotten into bed believing that you have done a great thing, one for which you deserve to have great praise heaped on you—and, of course, none comes. You have only done what everyone expects of you. You've gone a day without drinking; so what?

So you go through another day, and another. Somewhere along the line, you may sneak a drink, but basically, day after day, hour after hour, you resist. And then something happens, and you let down your guard and have a drink, and you may get away with it. The focus then is never on the week or two or even the month during which day after day, hour after hour, you stayed dry. No, the focus is on the slip. Once again, you have shown that you are not to be trusted. You have let everyone down—again.

The Finca incident had made one thing abundantly

clear. I was from then on, clearly, an alcoholic. "Hi, I'm Bill. I'm an alcoholic." Now 39, I wasn't going to be able to escape that stigma—which was the only way I could view it. The most obvious fallout was that I had to face up to a life without any drinking. Avowed alcoholics are told they can't work on a cutting-back plan. They have to swear alcohol off—completely and publicly. And that's what I did. I wasn't forced to make an announcement. I didn't have to wear a scarlet "A" on my jackets. But every time, anywhere, when anyone asked me what I wanted to drink, I had to ask for something nonalcoholic. The preferred response to "May I have a big glass of soda water, please?" is "Sure." But you would be surprised (or at least I was) by how many people tried to jolly me into something "more interesting." Some hosts were downright pushy. "Aw, come on, Bill, you can do better than that. How about a G&T? Or at least a nice glass of wine."

It is hard for anyone to understand what it meant to me to acknowledge that I would have to face a life sentence of complete abstinence. As I saw myself, alcohol was part of what defined me. I had been known as a bon vivant from my early days at the Bar Harbor Club, and all through school and college. It was an image I welcomed. Appreciation of fine wine and other strong drink was part and parcel of who I thought I was. I cried as I tried to explain to Louisa that I would no longer be me without alcohol.

That the lively, gregarious rascal she had married would be killed off and replaced by his dull, lifeless shell. Her reply was that in fact, the drunk or even somewhat tipsy me was not nearly as interesting a companion as my entirely sober self. It was the drunk me that became boring, not the lively sober one. Louisa had told me this many times. But that was a characterization of the situation I was simply not able to accept.

I was faced with a conundrum. How to preserve the mantle of bon vivant who knew about and appreciated the finer things in life, and still be known as a non-drinker? One device I adapted was to preserve for myself the luxury of "tasting" wine at dinner. Consider the serious wine tasters. They roll a little wine around in their mouth, allow a bit to trickle down their throat, and then spit out the rest. That small amount they swallow is enough to allow them to savor the wine to its fullest. Surely that approach would give me the best of both worlds. I could appreciate the fine wine as fully as professional wine tasters, while actually swallowing only the tiniest bit, thus never being in the slightest danger of having too much.

It is remarkable what kind of trouble just "tasting" wine can lead to. It really isn't that I drank too much by having an inch or even two inches of wine in my glass to "taste" during the course of a dinner. (It goes without saying that I always tried to make it two ounces, not one.) The problem was that even that small amount of wine would trigger a desire for more that lurks in some deep, devious part of my alcoholic brain.

There is no doubt that the permission I gave myself to taste wine made it easier for me to take the next step. Here's the situation: I've been sober a month—or three. Dinner is over. I am turning out the downstairs lights, just before going up to bed; Louisa has preceded me upstairs. Emboldened by my ounce or two of wine at dinner, and eager for the "click" I first experienced years earlier at St. Paul's, I hurriedly open the door to the liquor closet and swiftly, adroitly, surreptitiously uncork or unscrew a bottle. In no more than the blink of an eye, I take one long pull from its neck before quickly closing up both bottle and cabinet, and going on about my business, no one the wiser. But I had broken my stretch, however long it had been, of no drinking, and while I might be the only person to know, and while I would never tell, still I knew. Worse, it would be easier the next time. Yes, Louisa would sometimes smell alcohol on my breath, which I would vehemently deny. This routine mendacity, so characteristic of drinkers, was one of the most painful side effects of my addiction.

A real problem was that I was fooling myself. I was not really even trying to stop drinking entirely—that was simply much too hard and out of my reach. Deep down, all I aspired to was to keep my drinking my own private secret. This cat-and-mouse game with sobriety became the norm. I would try really hard to master my drinking, rather than stop drinking entirely.

I became a regular at the Chevy Chase Tuesday evening AA meeting. I would be proud as my period of sobriety lengthened. Sometimes, there would be some little slip that I could rationalize not reporting. It was so small that it really didn't count. But then something would happen, and I would give in, and the amount I drank would cross from what I could control into the area where I was no longer in charge. I would drink enough that Louisa would catch me, and then I would be in disgrace again, and the long climb to an honorable period of sobriety would begin anew.

My drinking was devastating to Louisa's and my relationship. The attendant mendacity was particularly pernicious. My staying on the wagon was absolutely essential to Louisa's and my ongoing life together. So a slip, even the tiniest, was a big deal, and not something Louisa could, or should have been expected to, forgive. But since getting caught drinking anything at all was going to cause major damage to our relationship, I had to avoid being caught at all costs. That meant lying. I pretty much had to be caught red-handed with a bottle to my mouth, or be falling-down drunk, before I was going to admit I had slipped. And since the increasingly watchful Louisa had developed an excellent nose for alcohol, and was by now finely attuned to other signs of my drinking as well, I would regularly be protesting my bone-dry condition and exemplary behavior when it was perfectly clear to her that I had been drinking—and was therefore lying again.

## 15

# BRUSSELS–
# A GENTLEMAN SPY

THERE FOLLOWED AN UNTENABLE PERIOD, WHERE my public position was that the incident at The Finca had taught me that I couldn't drink at all, but secretly I drank at work pretty much as before. It was time to leave the Operations Center. I had stayed on longer than the usual stretch and I was eager for a change. In the summer of 1974, I was posted to Brussels to work, not in the embassy, but in our Mission to the European Communities.

The Foreign Service isn't an obvious career choice for a Harvard MBA, and you might think I would have gravitated to the economic side at the State Department. But as political officers have always been acknowledged to be State Department elite, I felt I had to be a political officer.

Still, I often worked on economic issues and regularly found myself tapped for political jobs that had a heavy economic component. An anomaly of State Department staffing was that energy issues were classified under the political rubric, so when Joe Greenwald, U.S. ambassador to the European Communities, was casting about for a political officer to cover the European Community's energy policy, he saw the Harvard MBA on my CV and settled on me. It was a pretty good job.

I preceded Louisa to Brussels by two weeks, and camped out until she joined me in a handsome house, well located, on the edge of the Bois de la Cambre that we had found on an exploratory trip some months before. When I arrived, its furnishings consisted of one bed, one chair, and one table, all solicitously provided by the general services officer of the embassy. These were to carry me over until Louisa and our household effects arrived.

That put me in a situation which, for a short period of time, I could enjoy. If I wanted to go to the refrigerator the moment I got home from the office and make myself a nice gin and tonic—heavy on the gin—then sit in my chair and drink it, no one would say me nay. And when the first one was finished, I could make another if I wanted, and I wouldn't be letting anyone down. Drinking wasn't bad. All that was bad was having so much that it kept me from getting on with my life. On my own, in my spartanly furnished bachelor digs, I would see to it that that didn't happen. Make no mistake—I missed Louisa and the rest of the family tremendously, and welcomed them with open arms when they arrived. But until then, I had permission to be bad. Remember, being bad was one of my tricks.

Louisa and I never really took to Brussels. When we were assigned there, people told us we would love it. "It's only three hours down the auto route to Paris." When did anyone ever say the reverse regarding Brussels and a Paris posting? Another problem for us, and one that proved critical, was that while our thirteen-year-old daughter Eliza was with us, the boys, Bill and Nick, seventeen and fifteen, had stayed behind in boarding school. No matter how the rest of our lives had gone, the absence of the boys would have left us feeling only half there. But aside from that, even though we lived in a lovely house on the edge of the woods and had lots of friends, with some of whom we are still close, we were never excited about living in Brussels.

My drinking took on a somewhat different form in Brussels. I did not have quite the same regular daily intake that had come to characterize my work day in Washington. Working for the U.S. Mission to the Communities was a curious job. The US was not a member of the European Community, so we were not privy to its secret deliberations. However, information about what went on behind those closed doors was exactly what my government wanted me to provide. So I became an amateur spy. My job was to report to Washington the inner workings of the European Community (EC) relating to energy policy. It was expected that I would go around town chatting up everyone engaged in formulating energy policy and picking their brains. And that's what I did. By far, the best way to learn what was going on, however, was to get hold of the relevant classified European Community documents. I couldn't go snooping around, breaking into safes or tapping phone lines, so I had to find another solution. My approach was to cultivate people. I established friendships with people who had access to the documents I sought and who might be persuaded to share them with a friendly American colleague.

My best source was my counterpart in the U.K. Mission dealing in energy issues. He had easy access to everything I wanted, but he was also subject to the British Official Secrets Act. Happily, we both played squash and our regular matches brought us together, and we became good friends. He saw early on how helpful he could be to me and he saw no particular harm in sharing certain position papers with his American buddy. Sometimes it even helps if your negotiating partner knows your position. Many were the heavy plain brown envelopes passed from a member of the U.K. delegation dealing with energy issues to his U.S. colleague in the steamy locker room of the Brussels Squash and Tennis Club. A major advantage of using my U.K. colleague as a source was that documents I obtained from him were in English. Sometimes, however, and regrettably for me, for reasons best known to him, my English friend would demur. Yes, there had been a meeting, and yes, it had resulted in a juicy minute on probable next steps, but no, he didn't think he could see his way clear to letting me see that one, let alone handing it over. "Ten all, isn't it? Your serve." And that was that.

My next-best source was a Swiss official. He and I were in the same boat—both outsiders. Whereas I had a usually reliable British source, he could generally rely on his French colleagues to provide him the documents he needed. Anything my Swiss friend and co-conspirator got he was only too willing to share with me—and vice versa. The problem was that everything I got from him needed to be translated—not word for word, not the whole thing, but the key parts. That was time-consuming and inconvenient.

There were other sources. Two of the best-informed people in the whole Brussels community were two beautiful young Italian sisters, Lidia and Marina Gazzo, whose father published a daily newsletter reporting everything that had gone on in official EC organs during the preceding twenty-four hours. I do not think there was a senior bureaucrat in the entire official establishment in Brussels who did not pick up Gazzo's gazette first, even before the daily paper. To me, the Gazzo sisters were generous to a fault with information. They would willingly share a kir at the end of the day and fill me in on the goings on of the Community—but never with documents. I understood completely, and never pushed them beyond their comfort zone.

Finally, I had friends in the secretariat of the European Commission. One Dutchman in particular was my source of last resort, good from time to time, when I was in a pinch, for an especially well-protected document of which each copy was numbered. I think he shared because he liked the cloak-and-dagger overtones of doing so. I had the impression that when we met clandestinely he dressed the part, in his very best blue suit, crisp white shirt, subtle dark tie, and highly polished shoes.

I go into this aspect of my daily work because it reveals a difference in how I spent my lunch periods, which had direct bearing on my drinking habits. In Brussels, I had to cultivate a large number of potential sources of information. Therefore, my downfall in other jobs, the solitary liquid lunch, had no place in this new environment. My calendar was packed with lunch engagements with potential sources of information. I would drink wine with my lunch, of course, but no more than my guest. I didn't want the reputation of a tippler.

I found myself in a sort of no-man's-land. We were post-Finca. That incident had made it clear that I simply couldn't drink. Yet here I was, a Foreign Service officer in a position where I couldn't really do my job without drinking. I tried to devise, and then stick to, a sort of compromise position. I took as a given that I had to be seen to be a social drinker. I know now that that was not true. "I'll have a Perrier, please," is a perfectly acceptable response to "What can I get you to drink?" But I didn't know that then. Or perhaps I didn't want to know it. So the drinking regime changed in Brussels. The one place I was allowed to drink in Brussels was right out in the open. "Of course he's drinking. He is a diplomat." It went without saying that I should be known to be a drinker. It was OK to be a light drinker. At home, in private, I was a non-drinker.

There was no way this hybrid regimen was going to work for long, but it somehow got me through. Surprisingly, I, the prolific bottle-hider and secret-nipper, pretty well dropped that behavior. What got me into trouble was that I couldn't control my social drinking. At a business lunch, I could stick to a glass of wine. But at a dinner party, I found it hard to stick to a bottle. This was very hard on Louisa. She never knew which husband was going to take her home. Would the well-mannered, civilized, sober one get in the car, or would it be the one who was right on the edge of acceptable behavior, if not way over the line?

Drink entered the picture in another way. I was the officer in our mission who was charged with following the activities of the European Parliament. This body was advisory and had very little power, but it met regularly, debated weightily, and passed heady resolutions that would have been important had they ever become law. The parliament had a split personality, meeting half the time in Strasbourg and half the time in Luxembourg. I had to follow it to its respective haunts about once a month. Louisa was teaching and had Eliza to care for, so she never accompanied me; I was on my own. Here was where I could catch up on my solitary drinking.

One aspect of the parliament's business was that little of it was conducted behind closed doors. I didn't need to cultivate friends in my spare time to be able to know what was going on. People gave speeches and were glad to distribute the full text. Under these conditions, not only could I indulge in some solitary lunchtime drinking, but my hotel would always have a nice quiet bar where the tired bureaucrat could down a few nightcaps before bed. That may not seem very exciting, but it suited this problem drinker very well.

Two things happened in Brussels that broke the mold and tarnished the whole experience. The first was that I got drunk and had a bad automobile accident. Louisa was off on a jaunt with Eliza during her spring vacation, touring literary England for a few days and leaving me in Brussels, where I might get myself into mischief. What did me in was a night of too-heavy solitary drinking. Late at night, I was driving home from a quiet bar. I remember quite clearly the care with which I looked into the rearview mirror to make sure the way behind me was clear as I changed lanes and merged into a traffic circle. The problem was that with all of my attention focused behind me, I drove into a wall at the entrance to a mini-tunnel. I was driving a Volkswagen bus, and not wearing a seatbelt. My face hit the windshield hard, and my chest hit the steering column.

It was a big deal. I broke my sternum, four front teeth, and my jaw, and nearly bit off my tongue. Louisa felt entirely betrayed, because at my insistence, no one in my office let her know what happened. But after no word from me for several days, she became increasingly alarmed, and demanded that my secretary tell her what was going on. When she learned the facts, she and Eliza rushed home to find me in the hospital, covered in bruises, barely able to talk or laugh due to the excruciating pain from my broken sternum, and having to drink liquids through a straw. I was lucky in that an excellent U.S. Army oral surgeon, a trauma specialist who had served in Vietnam, postponed his leave to stay in Brussels long enough to put me back together, and I healed as well as could be expected. I still don't have all the feeling in my tongue, however, and I could have bought a Mercedes with what I have spent on related dental work over the years.

A second event cast a pall on our time in Brussels. In a midnight call, the rector of St. Paul's reported that our seventeen-year-old son Bill had said that he wasn't doing the school any good, nor it him, and that he was going to leave school and crash at the YMCA in Boston. Superficially, Bill had been doing fine. He was an officer of his class and the captain of a couple of teams, but he was using some dangerous, mind-bending drugs and not in good shape. The rector, terrified that this disturbed young man risked killing himself on school grounds, wanted to move him as far from the campus as possible. "That seems like a plan to me," he said of Bill's harebrained scheme. So much for *in loco parentis*. It was every parent's nightmare. We shortened our stay in Brussels by a year and returned home to cope. Bill's situation straightened itself out and he graduated from St. Paul's with his class and after a couple years off went to Johns Hopkins where he excelled.

Coming back to the Department in a hurry wasn't the best way to get a good new posting. I had to grab what was available. One interesting job offer did surface when an old friend who had just been named ambassador to Luxembourg asked me to be his deputy. We had just broken an assignment, in order to address a family crisis back home, so heading right back out wasn't an option. I settled for a job with our delegation negotiating the Law of the Sea Treaty, an assignment back in Washington that brought its own problems.

Reflecting on my drinking history, I marvel at my good fortune. The car accident was—miraculously—the only time my drinking resulted in any serious physical damage or injury. I can't even bear to consider what horrific additional harm I might have caused to myself, or others.

## 16

# TREADING WATER IN WASHINGTON

GIVEN THE QUICK DEPARTURE FROM BRUSSELS, the job I found looked good. I was assigned to be the executive secretary of the Interagency Task Force on the Law of the Sea (LOS) negotiations. (It sounded much more interesting and glamorous than it turned out to be.) We were going to change the world. After generations of chaos on the oceans, we were going to establish order—we were creating nothing less than the Law of the Sea. And, as the officer in charge of coordinating the interagency input for our negotiating position, I figured I would be in the thick of things.

The job had its good points. There were times when it looked like we might actually get a treaty; but the stars were badly aligned. First, when I arrived, we had terrible leadership. The titular head, the chief negotiator, was a political appointee who neither knew or really cared about the substance of the negotiations. His fine-sounding title gave him the standing to hobnob in senior Washington and international circles, and that's what he liked—and did. He left the negotiations to others.

The office space for the Office of the LOS was split up. Our chief negotiator did not share the space of the delegation on the fifth floor. No, he held out for, and got, a small office on the seventh floor, home of the secretary of state and other senior brass. "The seventh floor" was not just a way to designate space; it described elevated importance. "He works on the seventh floor," meant a person either was, or worked near, power. The fifth-floor offices, where the work on the negotiations got done, was presided over by an office director; a sound man, competent, but not a star. The primary role of the fifth floor LOS operation was to coordinate the positions of the various stakeholders in Washington into a coherent U.S. position. We had some good people doing good work, but no real leader. Still, we also had some sound contributors in the other agencies, and many of those working on the Law of the Sea had religion: We thought we were doing God's work. It was infectious.

About halfway through my tour, a development occurred that seemed most promising: Elliot Richardson was named to replace our politico as chief U.S. negotiator. We were delighted. Here was a four-time cabinet member, including secretary of defense, who had ample credentials. He was best known as the attorney general who had refused to carry out President Nixon's order to fire Watergate Special Prosecutor Archibald Cox. Richardson was a Washington hero. With someone like that at the helm, we might actually get an LOS agreement after all.

I remember Richardson's arrival at our office clearly. Tall, slim, patrician, very much in charge from minute one. He had with him three much younger men, one of whom, as it turned out, I would work with very closely—but I didn't know them then: Dick Darman, C.E. Smith, and an FSO I will call Harold Haskell. Richardson did all the talking. He asked questions of everyone in turn. Good questions. He wanted to know what the office really did. He saved the office director for last, and mostly wanted to discover from him how that office fit into the whole, how it interfaced with what was to be Richardson's office on the seventh floor, how it interfaced with the rest of the building, and finally, with the rest of Washington.

Then he turned to leave. When he was half in and half out of the room, and still had one hand on the door, he dropped what seemed like a bomb in that little suite of offices. "Harold Haskell (name changed) will stay here and head up this little operation. C. E., Dick, and I will settle in on the Seventh Floor." With that he swept out, his three minions in his wake. Haskell went too, though he came back before the day was out.

"This little operation" was in turmoil. The upshot of Richardson's closing remark was that our boss had just been fired. He hadn't been the most astute of bosses, but he was agreeable and didn't get in the way of getting the work done. The appointment of Haskell as our immediate boss was an enigma—most of us were prepared to wait and see. We were still riding high over the arrival of Elliot Richardson.

Though staff members were calm enough, our former boss was livid. Not only had he been summarily canned in front of his whole team, but perhaps worse, he had felt insulted when the office he headed, and of whose role he was justifiably proud, had been dismissed as "this little operation."

It was an edgy bunch that greeted Haskell when he came back into the office, unannounced, about ten minutes before quitting time that afternoon. He didn't have the chutzpah to use the still-present boss's office, but nearly. The first person he wanted to talk to was his new number two, but before they closeted themselves in the deputy's office, he made a list of the people he wanted to see next, and the order in which he wanted to see them. It was past quitting time, but we were clearly settling down to a long night. We were all professionals, and often gladly stayed late for the cause—sometimes very late. But there were necessary rituals that had not been observed. There had been no "please" or "thank you." No brief explanation of why a late night was needed. Only an assumption that if he was working, we would be also. Haskell spent an hour cloistered with his new deputy and then spent fifteen minutes to a half hour with each of the dozen or so others in the office. It was about ten in the evening when he was finished, and he was irritated that no secretary had been kept on through the night to whom he could dictate his notes.

This kind of behavior dominated Haskell's reign. He prided himself on his late hours, and he didn't like to work alone. Often, he would be working on a paper behind closed doors, but he wanted "you," "you," and "you" to stick around until "we can get this thing out." He could stay cloistered for over an hour with a team at the ready just in case they might be needed.

Because of the nature of my position, I would necessarily work closely with Haskell. My title was a mouthful: staff director of the National Security Council (NSC) Interagency Group (IG) for the Law of the Sea. The job had two quite separate responsibilities, both related to the large number of stakeholders. Carving out the U.S. government position involved, for starters, getting agreement among seventeen member agencies, eight congressional committees, and other miscellaneous entities in order to arrive at an agreed U.S. position to bring to the LOS Conference. This conference was made up of 150 countries and other groups. Its mandate was huge: To negotiate a framework for exploitation of marine resources, air and sea navigation, control of pollution, maritime scientific research, and compulsory settlement of disputes.

Organizationally, I was not under the State Department but under the NSC—the National Security Council. As the staff director of the Interagency Group, I was responsible for its day-to-day coordination and operation, scheduling negotiations within the U.S. government to find a unified position. As staff director, I sat right at the center of things, keeping track of the whole, not just particular parts. I prepared a lot of briefing books—including preparing ("singlehandedly," according to my efficiency report) the briefing books for both of Secretary Kissinger's appearances at the conference. I also chaired a lot of interagency meetings. Shortly after Richardson was named chief negotiator, I represented the United States at an important intercessional meeting in Geneva.

This job was more demanding than most in that the amount of detail the incumbent—in this case, me—had to juggle in his head was considerable. For the first time, I became quite compulsive about controlling my drinking.

It was not so much that I wanted to reduce my intake, but I did want to pace myself more rigidly than heretofore. Up to now, I had been fairly casual about timing my forays to my bottles and about the amount I would take per stop. This time, I made a little schedule to the minute. In no way did this mean I could always follow it, but it did give me something to shoot for, and something to use as a control. Similarly, I stopped allowing myself to take especially large swallows just because I felt like it. I timed my libations as a patient times his meds. What made my behavior different from before was that this time I had my consumption all written down, and I was determined to stick to it. There was a drink on the morning commute, then the pre-lunch, the lunch, after lunch, mid-afternoon (I also called that one "tea"), quitting time, and finally the commute-home drink.

There was another side to drinking while working on the Law of the Sea. We did a certain amount of traveling to the United Nations' headquarters in New York and the headquarters in Geneva. Travel is convenient for the married drinking man. The long gap between the end of one work day, and the beginning of the next, with no one to suggest you shouldn't order another carafe of wine to go with the cheese, was a plus.

I didn't think much about my drinking regime at the time; that was just how I got through the day. Looking back,

I find it quite remarkable that I could stick to a system like that. I, who, when I was home, could not be relied on not to drink too much and embarrass my wife and children. The two types of drinking seem to serve quite different purposes. The highly regimented drinking during the day is not really done for pleasure. It is what I had to do to get through the day. Having too much at home at dinner, or at a party, is quite another thing. That is something I looked forward to and enjoyed. It was part of the good life.

Haskell never got any better, and as time went on I realized one of his problems. He was inordinately jealous of C.E. Smith, who, you will remember, had settled in with Richardson and Darman on the seventh floor. Haskell said he could accept that Richardson wanted the other member of the triumvirate, Dick Darman, at his side. "Darman is the smartest man I know," Haskell had confided to me in a weak moment, "but what's Smith doing up there? I'm smarter than he is." (Darman went on to head the Office of Management and Budget (OMB), under President George H. W. Bush, but even he couldn't straighten the budget out.)

It's a pity, but the LOS treaty never lived up to its promise. It was concluded in 1982 and came into force in 1994, and has been signed by over 150 countries. It has become accepted international law. But the US never ratified it and is not a party to it. That step has consistently been blocked by conservatives who object to one of its principles, that minerals on the deep seabed are common property—the "common heritage of mankind." Richardson was impressive, and Richardson and Darman together were awesome. But even they couldn't beat down the conservative opposition.

## 17

## SERVING MANY MASTERS
## IN WASHINGTON

MY TIME AT LAW OF THE SEA CAME TO AN END, AND Louisa and I were hoping for another Washington assignment. When the job of Benelux desk officer was offered, I snapped it up. Desk officer is a quintessential Foreign Service job. The desk officer for a big country like Japan or Germany would have several officers under him. On the other hand, several smaller countries might share a single desk officer. That would be my situation as Benelux desk officer, covering Belgium, The Netherlands, and Luxembourg from Washington, D.C. For each country, I would have two constituencies: My primary job would be to act as the conduit between my client embassies in Washington and the State Department. But our embassies in those three foreign capitals also would have a claim on my time. I would be their gofer for everything relating to the Washington bureaucracy.

Being Benelux desk officer was a good job for me in several ways. My six embassies—two in each of the three countries—each clamored for attention, and sent me scurrying all over the Department and throughout the U.S. government on their service. Much of what I did was of the putting-out-fires variety. My daily to-do list generally consisted of a dozen projects with deadlines that day or the next. The constant interaction with people seemed to help keep me away from the bottle.

Perhaps even more to the point, I had a hands-on boss who kept close tabs on what his subordinates were doing. The upshot was that my usual routine of getting a little drunk at lunch didn't work very well. Not only was I going to be seeing people all throughout the afternoon, I had a boss who would have noticed if I were drunk. (I find it remarkable that this was the exception, not the rule, in the Department.)

Most importantly, I made a huge decision. I really was going to quit all drinking at work. I had been encouraged by how well I seemed to have been able to control my intake under my earlier minute-by-minute, ounce-by-ounce regime. It was time to take the next step. I had to go beyond controlling my drinking; I had to stop it. On the job and off. I had again begun to go regularly to AA meetings, which I was finding helpful. I partially bought into the AA creed. I could admit that I was an alcoholic and, as such, I had no power to control my drinking. I tried to accept that I could not drink just a little; could not sip wine at dinner, nor drink the birthday toast. I had to stop. I took pride as my days of sobriety turned to weeks, then months. But it became harder and harder, until one day it would become too hard and I would slip. Most of the time a slip was a slip. If I sneaked some drinks that no one but me knew about, that was a slip. It didn't matter if it broke a dry spell of three days, or weeks or even months; a slip set the clock back to zero. But what if no one but me knew it? What if I really had gotten away with it? I admit, in shame I still feel, that more than once I failed to admit the secret slip to anyone and continued to pretend I was still on a dry spell.

It is hard to get people never afflicted with a strong addiction to really understand how powerful the need to succumb is. True, I wanted to lick the problem. I wanted to be cured. However it was equally true that I wanted to drink pretty much every minute of every day. Still, my time on the Benelux desk was one of the periods where I tried hardest to kick my habit, and came the closest to it.

My work on sobriety began when I got into my little blue secondhand Fiat to drive to work. I would think of the perfect little hidey-hole below the rubber flap under the driver's seat: the perfect place to hide a half pint of vodka—but now empty. As I drove down Rock Creek Parkway towards the Department, I would yearn for the little swigs I used to take from that bottle. All morning long I would ache knowing that lunch was not going to bring relief. No little trips to my parked car. Not even little bottles with my lunch. I still often lunched alone and in my habitual restaurants, and my abstinence was remarked on by my habitual servers. Some just dropped a little comment, but some wanted the whole story. Was I quitting for good? Why? I gave them the brief version. I said that it seemed like a good idea at the time.

The need to drink would increase as the afternoon wore on. As I left the building at the end of the day, I was acutely aware of the fact that apart from the little liquor store right across the street from the State Department entrance I used, there were two other liquor stores not two blocks away. Getting a fresh half pint would be the work of an instant. But I would refrain. Once home, the temptation continued. The liquor cabinet was always filled to the brim with a wide variety of forbidden bottles—wasn't that part of the good life? Hour after hour, day after day, night after night, I would somehow refuse to drink.

Then something would happen. I would never know what might set me off, but after all the holding back, all the saying no, I would sneak a drink—and lightning would not strike. I would get that lovely little click in the back of my head that I so craved, but then I was able to stop. Nobody but me knew I had had a little slip. So soon after, I would try it again—and then again. Then, of course, one day I would go too far and Louisa would either smell the alcohol, or worse, recognize the symptoms of my drinking. I would protest—and lie. But it was no good. It was clear once again that I had not stopped. That I was still drinking. That I could not be trusted.

That was all true. I had not stopped and could not be trusted. But only the drinker knows how many times he has controlled that terrible urge. How many hours, days, and weeks he went with no slip at all, not a drop, not even a sniff. And he feels all that effort is not appreciated—not recognized. All anyone—everyone, he thinks—knows is that once again, he has had a drink.

I would go to AA and fess up, admitting a slip. Great sympathy all around. No condemnation. Much discussion: What had caused it? What to do to prevent a recurrence? And a new dry spell would begin. Dry days would be tallied—a week, then two, then a month. But it never got any easier.

Moreover, I got into the habit of lying to myself. I have reported that I really was trying to solve my drinking problem. That's very true. Deep down I knew that I had to nearly give it up or it would continue to get away from me, making my life miserable. However, I always preserved and cherished my ace in the hole. I had quit, yes. I could not drink at home or out to dinner or anywhere. We all understood that, even me. But what I knew and no one else did was that I still had my little reservation in place. When I was on my own for a few days (and it was bound to happen from time to time), when the house was empty—then I would be able to slip back into a more normal, more civilized mode. I would be able to have a few solitary drinks. Not enough to get me into any trouble. Not enough for anyone to even know. Just enough to Put Things Right with the world for a few days. It was something to look forward to.

I fear I'm painting too rosy a picture. I've acknowledged above that I would slip—that I was not reliable. When I did slip, the consequences would vary. Sometimes, they would not be great. I would sneak a swig at Saturday lunch at home, but would have a little nap after lunch, and be more or less OK for the rest of the afternoon or evening.

Sometimes, however, things got out of hand. With a fair regularity I had to get dressed up and grace someone's grand diplomatic function. These events could be dangerous for my drinking. I was apt to try to get a swallow or two in me before heading out of the house, just for fortification. Then, as drinks were passed before dinner, empties were promptly refilled. Refills were prompt all through dinner. By the end of dinner I would often be sailing toward troubled water. Most of the time I would be OK to an untutored eye, and I would go home perhaps in Louisa's bad graces, but my cover as a serious mid-level diplomat was intact.

Not always, though. Sometimes I would go too far and become noticeably drunk. Consider, for example, the Chopin evenings offered regularly by Luxembourg Ambassador Meisch. U.S.-Luxembourg relations were not the stuff of high drama. It wasn't until 1956 that Luxembourg rated its own American ambassador. Until then the US was represented in Luxembourg by our envoy in either Belgium or The Netherlands. In my time, however, Luxembourg rated its own ambassador, and Ambassador Meisch did what was necessary to keep business with the US ticking along smoothly. What he was best known for in Washington were his charming musical evenings. He was an accomplished pianist and he held regular soirees consisting of a reception, followed by his concert and then dinner. These were very civilized affairs and Louisa and I were regular attendees.

I have said that I could not be trusted not to overdo my drinking in public. At one of Ambassador Meisch's musical evenings, I let down the team. I sneaked something to drink at lunch, enough so that I was not entirely sober when I woke up from a nap. Louisa, fearing the worst, wanted me to call in sick but I got stubborn and insisted on going. That was typical behavior. I would have been very happy to beg off, and I did recognize that I was too drunk to go. I didn't want Louisa to be the one to tell me that, however, so we suited up in our best bib and tucker and went. Not surprisingly, I had more to drink during the pre-concert reception, which pretty much guaranteed I would sleep through the Chopin. That didn't matter much, however. I was in pretty good company. Lots of guests did some snoozing.

The next challenge was the dinner. The guest list for an affair like this was a hodgepodge of the most important people the embassy could round up. Mid-level people from the European Bureau of the State Department, people from other U.S. government agencies with which Luxembourg has business, the diplomatic corps, and miscellaneous local dignitaries made up the guest list. (Some of this latter category managed to be on several embassy guest lists and freeload regularly.) I got through dinner without a major mishap, and we took our leave as soon as it was polite to do so.

I mention this incident because it is fairly typical. I got drunk and I had some interactions at dinner. But I was compos mentis enough making my goodbyes. I think it's possible Ambassador Meisch didn't even notice anything untoward about my formulaic farewell remarks. On the other hand, I would be very surprised if my dinner partners failed to mention to their husbands that their dinner partner, a guy from the State Department, got drunk.

So what of it? I had gotten drunk, but not so drunk that anyone who counted—other than Louisa—knew it. That's what happened often. I would have a slip, but no one—other than Louisa—would know it. The gingerbread man would have gotten away with it again. But, of course, he had not.

## 18

## SAILING AWAY MY MIDLIFE CRISIS

MY MIDLIFE SAILING ADVENTURE IS CERTAINLY ONE illustration of my self-indulgence. It is also an occasion when, once again, I saw how remarkably wonderful Louisa is.

I was restless. It's hard for me from this remove to pinpoint what it was about my life that made me yearn for a change so passionately, but something did. Maybe I just wanted to run away for a while. I was in my mid-forties. Isn't that a vulnerable age? I began to dream of the South Seas. I reread *Pitcairn's Island.* Then all of the *Bounty* trilogy. Then all of Nordhoff and Hall. I was hooked. I couldn't go to the Pacific—too far—but why not take a little turn through islands of the Caribbean? I began to read up on them. What started as a daydream began to take form. This was something I might really do.

I finally dared to broach the idea with Louisa. We had, of course, shared our fantasies over the years. Mine of sailing into the sunset, off for a cruise, not a lifetime. Hers of buying an apartment in Paris on the sunny bank of the Ile Saint-Louis and finishing out her years as a little old lady in tennis shoes. But I was beginning to get serious about mine. Of course, Louisa was invited. But realistically speaking, we both always knew that she would not come. First off, she does not share my huge irresponsible streak. She doesn't like to be out of sight of land. She had a new PhD that she was eager to begin using as a teacher. But most importantly, we couldn't both abandon the kids like that. We were parents, for heaven's sake. Even with the kids away at college, they needed care and feeding, someone had to guard the nest. If I went, it would be without Louisa.

I will never really understand why Louisa was so supportive, but I love her for it. Of course, she realized I was as much running away from something as toward anything. But I think she saw, as no one else did, how much I wanted to do this. In any event, she said she didn't want to come, but that she understood my need and she was behind me. I had been attending AA, and had been dry for months. If Louisa worried, it was more about danger at sea than about my drinking.

We looked at the charts and made some calculations. I said I thought it would take five months to do it right, and Louisa said OK. The hurricane season is generally considered to be over by November 30. We decided I would start in early December. I got permission from the State Department to take a leave of absence and began to plan in earnest.

From the very beginning, I had alcohol on my mind. From the days of hiding beer on the A boat for the July cruise, I had often taken some beer along on sails, sometimes more than was prudent. It seemed very natural to look around the boat for a place to keep a little stash. Sailing off alone, leaving the usual constraints that were restricting my drinking behind, was taking a risk—it would leave me vulnerable. Drinking too much could absolutely kill this project. I would have to be very careful. In my favor was the fact that my head was in a pretty good place. At this stage, I was believed by my friends to have quit drinking. At parties, I would have soda water. At meals, I wanted a wine glass, but with only a splash of wine in the bottom. *Une larme* (a tear). Still, even under my boss's watchful eye, I would often get a swig or two during the workday. At home, I was almost dry, but it doesn't mean there wasn't still a bottle tucked around the cellar, known only to me. I was determined, however, that drink would not ruin my sail. I made lots of private promises to keep my drinking under control, except for certain special occasions like major landfalls. I did make one hard and fast rule: Not a drop until the anchor was down, ever. That would be the bright line. What I did not do was swear off completely for the duration.

I am not sure why I thought I was in a position to draw any line. I had certainly not yet demonstrated that I could control my drinking, or show that I was in charge. But there had been periods during which, with the help of AA, I had been able to refrain from drinking for weeks and even months at a time. I drew on those dry periods for the confidence that I could control my drinking during the sail. That, and the certain knowledge that if I did not control my drinking, the whole sailing adventure would end in some sort of disaster or tragedy.

I was rather cavalier about choosing a boat. It's my nature to go off half-cocked and I didn't really research the purchase as thoroughly as I might have. Doing so would have saved me some money, but I am not sure I could have found a better boat for my purposes. I bought a Westsail 32, a gorgeous thirty-two-foot double-ended cutter. A cutter has one mast, stepped fairly far aft so as to permit both a staysail and a jib forward. I chose that rig because it is simple to single-hand. I got a small boat for the same reason. Small, yes, but really seaworthy. The prototype of my boat was designed by the renowned Norwegian naval architect

Colin Archer to be a pilot boat, able to go out in anything. I wanted to be, and be seen by Louisa to be, safe. I named the boat *Mon Panache,* from the dying words of Cyrano de Bergerac who never lost his *panache*—literally his white plume, but really his flair for life. I fell for her the moment I saw her. She was salty, a real sailor's boat.

It was hard for me to admit that the next step was necessary, but good sense about a completely solo effort prevailed, to an extent. I engaged someone to sail with me for the first thousand-mile offshore leg of my sail: south from Florida, leaving the Bahamas to our west, and then sailing east, passing north of the Greater Antilles—Haiti, the Dominican Republic, Puerto Rico. Our first landfall was to be at Charlotte Amalie on St. Thomas in the U.S. Virgin Islands. From there, I would be on my own, island-hopping through the Leeward Islands and the Windwards, and down to the Grenadines off the coast of Venezuela.

I was a good hand on a boat. I had been sailing all my life, but almost exclusively in small boats—day sailors. Every night I put in to a harbor. True, I had logged a number of nautical miles on cruising boats of one sort or another, but it had all been as crew. I had no experience as skipper of anything bigger than thirty-foot knockabouts. Those were not much shorter than *Mon Panache,* but they were about a tenth the weight. The experience was entirely different. Moreover, I had never sailed in really heavy weather. When it blew too hard, I had always had the luxury of staying in port. On the passage I had planned, we would be at sea for up to two weeks at a stretch. No ducking into the nearest port in a blow. So for that long initial offshore hop, I needed a captain, someone with me who had some experience.

Tom, the guy I hired, was young, but he had made several "deliveries" from Florida to St. Thomas. The downside was he had always been crew, never a skipper. Still, he had much more offshore experience than I did; we would learn together, I argued, and our strengths would complement one another's. I also engaged him to take delivery of *Mon Panache* in Sarasota and do some of the initial outfitting. I was to come down a week before our departure, and we would go through sea trials together. Tom had a girlfriend, Susan, who he suggested come along as an unpaid crew member. He pointed out that sharing watches one on, one off was really hard; the third hand would be a big help. I agreed.

From a drinking standpoint, I decided to consider the outfitting period a sailing period—that would mean no booze. I stuck to that. We worked pretty hard. We had a lot to get ready. One real nuisance was that the new Yamaha diesel engine kept quitting. A mechanic I am not. Although I didn't expect to use the engine much—we would be under sail, for the most part—I certainly wanted it to work. (In the end, a new solenoid was all she needed, and we had no more problems.)

Louisa came down to Sarasota just before we sailed to see us off. She and I had fun fitting *Mon Panache* out with the non-nautical but essential homey things such as knives and forks, dishes, glasses, and towels. She bought me a wok, which was great for the sail and which we still use regularly at home. We were like newlyweds fitting out a small apartment, and it was romantic sleeping together on board. Then one bright sunny day, Tom, Susan—who was quite nice—and I cast off on schedule, waving to Louisa until she was out of sight. Seeing her disappear was a jolt and reminded me how remarkable—and how dear of her—it was for her to give this adventure her blessing.

I have reported that I was not drinking, and that I had a good attitude about staying sober, but I have been holding back a key piece. True, I wasn't planning to cut out booze entirely, but still, I couldn't imagine sailing off on a bone-dry ship. Tom and his girl had brought along such booze as they would need—a pint of rum. They both drank in moderation. I had been very clear that there were to be no controlled substances of any kind on board, and I thought we were clean that way, too.

Ironically, I was the one with the secret stash. I had emptied a two-liter plastic Sprite bottle and filled it up with light rum. I wasn't drinking, I told myself. I didn't plan to drink except on special, still-unidentified occasions, but I was ready for anything.

It turned out to be a very hard sail. It began with heavy weather down the west coast of Florida. Our plan was to go through the drawbridge at the town of Marathon to avoid going all the way around the Keys. Then we would proceed east to where we could pick up the trade winds, and then have a sleigh ride, as it were, down to the Virgins. It all sounded so easy. The first big glitch was that the wind in the Keys was so high, for so long, that we had to wait three days in Marathon for the bridge to be opened. We were no sooner through than the wind picked up again and we found ourselves breaking in our still-untried boat in fifteen-to-twenty-foot seas and thirty-five to forty knots of wind. Neither Tom nor I were comfortable about setting off under those conditions, so we changed course and ran for cover under the Bahamian island of San Salvador. Susan, who was pretty much constantly seasick, said she had had enough, so she abandoned ship and flew home. Happily, Tom got on the telephone and was able to find a young man he knew in Florida who was eager to make the trip. That kid, Patrick, who flew down for a small fee, turned out to be a great addition.

The weather stayed bad, however, and after a second attempt to clear the Bahamas we were again met by

near-gale winds and fifteen-to-twenty-foot seas, forc-
ing us to duck back in to another island for shelter. That
proved to be the straw that broke Tom's back; he, too,
announced that he had no stomach to finish the trip.
That really put it to me. I was reluctant to go on with just
Pat—the blind leading the blind. It was not clear to me
that I could finish if I couldn't get someone with some
experience to accompany me on the open water heading
to the Virgins.

I go into some detail about these problems because
they strike me as the sort of thing that could drive a man—
any man—to drink. Yet surprisingly, at no time in this very
messy and deeply discouraging period did I even really
consider either breaking out my secret Sprite bottle of rum
or slipping into one of the many watering holes on either
of the islands we were anchored by. I imagine what kept
me on the straight and narrow was the knowledge that if
I slipped at all, I would slip too far. If I was going to pull
the remainder of this sail out of the hat, I would have to be
solid, and that meant sober.

Throughout all these setbacks, I kept in close touch
with my most trusted voice—Louisa—via my reliable sin-
gle-sideband radio.It was she who came up with an excellent lead that produced a captain, a woman named Maria
who was willing and able to complete the trip. She arrived
in a couple of days, and we set off again.

The weather didn't improve. Most of the time, we had much too much wind, including a quite frightening three-day gale, but we were developing lot of faith in our sturdy *Mon Panache,* and we pushed on. Maria was a real pro. She had done this crossing several times and had lots of heavy weather experience. This time we just sailed through even the nastiest weather. Looking back, I realize the bad weather that Tom and I ducked was well within *Mon Panache*'s capabilities, but we were too green—and shaken up—to know that then.

We weren't even sailing alone. We had teamed up, as we left the Bahamas, with a forty-foot sloop called the *Blue Peter,* skippered by a guy named Harry who was also heading to Charlotte Amalie. We decided to cruise in company. It was a nice arrangement, and we felt more secure with the *Blue Peter* in sight or, in the gales, on the other end of the radio. Maria and Harry had gotten quite chummy on the radio, and Maria was looking forward to getting to know him in port. (In fact, they later got married.) I mention Harry and the *Blue Peter* here because Maria began to talk of the standard sailor's agenda, on reaching port: to get stewed, screwed, and tattooed. Everyone was talking about having a big blowout. I couldn't bear to be left out. I began to think about booze. I could at least get stewed.

And I did. The details are long lost, but I awoke the next morning not only hungover but still drunk. There were many things I needed to do of which I was incapable. Louisa, I have no doubt, has a better recollection than I of some of the details. At my mother's request (and expense!), Louisa had arranged for most of the extended family, including all of our kids, to spend the Christmas holidays at a charming resort in Nevis. I know I made an arrangement (or did Louisa make it?) to be flown from Charlotte Amalie to Nevis by a chartered plane, but I missed the rendezvous. I caught another plane, and did get to Nevis in time for Christmas, but it was of course a huge disappointment to Louisa to have me show up not only late, but somewhere between drunk and deadly hungover after such a long absence. I am so ashamed of myself, even after these many years, that I can barely bring myself to write about it. Louisa (the heroine of this saga, who deserved a triumphant reunion) wept all through the Christmas service at a local church the next day.

I returned to complete sobriety for the rest of the vacation on Nevis—but the damage had been done. At the end of the Nevis portion, Louisa flew right home to her teaching job (that had always been the plan) and the three kids stayed on for a bit. We had a short, delightful cruise together—dry.

The one other occasion during that sail when I had much too much to drink was in St. Barthélemy, commonly known as St. Barts. I don't know what got me started that time. I had just picked up a little Canadian family who were in need of help. They had decided to take the trip of a lifetime before they were too old to enjoy it; they had sold the husband's construction business and set off to drift on down through the islands for six months or so. They had backpacks adorned with jaunty Canadian flags, and a five-year-old and a two-year-old—who still sometimes demanded and got—"a booby" from Mom. They were going to sleep in fields and catch rides between islands on local boats. They had landed in St. Martin two weeks earlier and discovered that they couldn't camp anywhere and that food of any kind—and everything else—cost a fortune. I was just exploring St. Barts on foot when I came across the mom, Polly. She was sitting on the ground, crying her heart out. I can't resist a damsel in distress, so I stopped. Prompted, she poured out her sad story. They were hemorrhaging money, and at the present rate, the planned six-month trip would be cut to four weeks—at best. They would return home broke, humiliated, with their tails between their legs. I suggested that she send her husband to talk to me. Perhaps I could help. The upshot was that Joe did come see me and we worked out a temporary solution. They would move onto *Mon Panache* for a few days, where they could take a breather and plan next steps in peace and comfort.

Why in the world I picked that moment to break into my Sprite bottle I have no idea, but I did. No sooner did they move in than I began to take little nips, and then I went at it in earnest. I don't know when they began to notice, but when I came home late one night, there was no hiding it. In the morning, I explained all: I was an alcoholic who had been under control but had "slipped." I ceremoniously poured the rum overboard, and that was the end of it.

I was dry for the rest of the trip. I didn't even allow myself the occasional little something on shore from time to time. I would belly up to the bar and say in my best man-of-the-world voice, "Make me a fruit punch, please."

Louisa joined me during her spring break for a lovely little cruise through the Grenadines. I also left *Mon Panache* at anchor once and flew to Washington for a conjugal visit. Those little visits were highpoints of my sail. But there was no escaping the obvious. I had hoped to go off on that trip and come home having proved I could go without alcohol; I had proved just the opposite. I had failed the test. I had not even managed to stay sober when it mattered the most. Though I had been sober—dry—the vast bulk of the time, I couldn't be trusted.

# 19

## CALM CANADA

NOT LONG AFTER THE START OF MY SAIL, THE STATE Department began to bug me about my next assignment. The Department plans far ahead. The only way they could contact me was at our home address, through Louisa, who would relay to me the substance of their missives. The message was always the same: It was time for me to look over the upcoming postings available, and to list the ones that appealed to me in order of preference. The logistics of this were easier than it might appear. We had surprisingly many consular posts throughout the islands and they all had microfiches listing open positions. I just had to drop in at one and pick and rank three postings. Microfiches and ongoing assignments were what I was sailing away from, however, so I dragged my feet. Louisa finally got fed up with my procrastination. "Stop at a consulate," she said, "pick a post and be done with it. NOW!"

So I did. It was easy. I was in Martinique, so I made a rendezvous with the consul general there for the next day. In the morning I cleaned myself up a bit, put on my one pair of long pants and my only shoes, and kept my appointment. By mid-morning, I had picked three possibilities and ranked them. By the end of the day, the consul general had sent a telegram listing my choices. By week's end, Louisa informed me of the Department's decision: I was to stay in Washington, assigned to the Canadian desk. I don't remember where that had been on my list, but it suited me fine.

It was another desk job, like the Benelux desk, but very different. The Benelux desk had been a one-man show. I had been the sole officer on the desk, responsible for everything relating to my three small countries. The Canadian desk was another matter. In that case, a team of five officers shared the management of our relations with our giant northern neighbor, under the direction of a country director. My share of that task included both the energy and the fisheries sectors, arguably the two most important issues in our bilateral relationship in the early eighties. I was pleased to have subjects that promised to be meaty—so to speak.

As I returned to work after my five-month vacation, I was eager to do a good job. Even though my Christmas binge had badly blotted my copybook—an expression that dates from my pen-and-ink days in elementary school— most of the time I had been able to stay away from alcohol entirely, and that had given me the incentive to really try to hold my alcohol use in check. I was not ready to say to the world that Bill Newlin didn't drink. This was a huge step forward in my thinking about alcohol, however. I was going to try to get through every day, day after day, week after week, month after month, without any drinking. Nothing on the way to work. Nothing at lunch. Nothing on the way home. Nothing over the weekend. What made it possible for me to make that resolution, and to think I had a good chance of keeping it, was my little private reservation.

It would not be cheating to drink when I was left alone in the house for a day or two—or more. That was a very small escape clause I was giving myself. Looking back, I am surprised that it was as important to me as it was. Louisa and I were not apart very often or for very long. I wasn't hoping to change that. I wasn't even eagerly awaiting the announcement of some impending, early trip by one of us. It seems that that little reservation was all I required to give myself the illusion that I was not signing off drink completely, forever. I was not greedy. I could wait. Moreover, it didn't need to be a long separation. But I did have to know that my very fickle friend, alcohol, was not out of my life for good.

I fear that last paragraph suggests that I would welcome a life without Louisa—a life where I could drink pretty much to my heart's content. In fact, the exact opposite is true. What I wanted to preserve, above all else, was my relationship with Louisa, the love of my life. Drink threatened it. If I could sign off completely when we were together—if she could count on me not to be drunk at home at night or when we went out together, then alcohol would no longer threaten our relationship, or so I rationalized. Limiting my drinking to times we were apart killed two birds with one stone. I didn't have to sign off entirely—which I just couldn't do. But the drinking I did do, if it were limited to when we were apart, would not threaten our relationship because she would never know. All I had to do was stick to that regime.

I returned to AA. My old group was still meeting in the Chevy Chase Baptist Church, and I rejoined them. It felt like old home week, as if I hadn't been away. Many of them still remembered me. When it was my turn to take the floor—"Hi, I'm Bill, I'm an alcoholic"—I filled them in. I had taken some time off sailing. I had done pretty well with alcohol but had had some bad slips, and one terrible one. Now I wanted to quit for good. Some people clapped. I didn't tell them about my reservation. Didn't tell them I didn't really want to quit. Not all the way.

There was another thing I didn't tell them. I did not

tell them what I have confessed here—that during my earlier time with AA I had not fessed up to every little slip. AA makes a big deal of how long you have been sober. When you slip you go back to Go and start the count all over again at zero. I had cheated. Sometimes I would be claiming three months sober, but only I knew those three months had had four slips in them. I did not confess to this unethical behavior. I wanted their good will and support. But while I did not confess to my earlier cheating, I did forswear it. I promised myself that in the future, I would confess to any slip, no matter how small. A slip would set my clock back to zero.

I drifted in and out of AA. When I felt strong I would let it slide and then when I felt vulnerable I would return to the meetings. There's no doubt in my mind, however, that AA was a big help in keeping me sober. Louisa was very supportive of my AA attendance. First, because she took as an article of faith the premise that AA was a good thing for any alcoholic. She was always disappointed when I stopped going and glad when I picked it back up. But she also enjoyed the tales I would bring home. The world around us is filled with soap operas, but most of them are untold. People don't go around revealing all the quirky peculiarities of their lives, but that's how AA works. Drinking is all wound up with living life. You can't explain the drinking without talking about life. So week after week our group watched as the fascinating sagas of our fellow addicts unfolded. The most interesting of these tales I would relate to Louisa, who loves a good story—of course, using no names. I wonder if anyone was recounting my own stories, and to whom?

I fear I may be under-reporting the hold alcohol still had on me. I was not drinking very much—almost nothing. But that represented a ferocious struggle. I pretty much always wanted to drink.

I was not willing to alter the way I lived to reduce the temptations inherent in that lifestyle. We still kept our alcohol in a rather large cupboard in the pantry. The space had to be pretty copious because any well-appointed house had to be ready for even esoteric drink requests. It wasn't enough to have a single fortified wine, for example sherry—or even two—sherry and port. You also needed to have marsala and/or Madeira. One liqueur—perhaps crème de menthe—wasn't enough. You needed at least a bottle of Benedictine and one of Cointreau. Whiskies? Sure, bourbon and scotch, but how about an Irish, too? And on it went. That cupboard was right in plain sight and never locked—not even latched. I made sure it could be opened without making even the slightest sound.

I never walked by it without feeling the pull. How easy it would be. Everyone was in the living room. Out of sight of the pantry. I could open the door in a flash, grab the vodka, top shelf, right in the middle, take a big swig, screw the cap back on, bottle back in place, door shut. The whole thing wouldn't take as much as ten seconds and I would have that lovely warm feeling in my chest—and that little click wouldn't be far behind. But time after time, I resisted.

## 20

**NICE WAS NICE**

LIFE ON THE CANADIAN DESK, WHERE I SERVED from 1980 to 1983, had been pretty tame, and I was ready for a foreign assignment with some pizazz. Happily, personnel held out some hope. One job on the list of possible postings was that of consul general in Bordeaux. That would have suited me just fine. It would have brought us back to France, which would have pleased me and delighted Louisa. Even better, it would have made me my own boss. I was ready for that. But I had a problem: a personnel officer was ahead of me in line. It's an open secret that a perk of a tour in personnel is that you get to write your ongoing ticket. Having initially been told that Bordeaux was mine, I discovered that an officer in personnel had his sights on it for himself.

Nevertheless, I got lucky. The personnel office had another plum up its sleeve: the consulate general in Nice. It had been closed some years before as a cost-saving measure. Now there was pressure to reopen it. Were that to happen, I was told, I would get it. Nice was a smaller post. But the allure of the Riviera was not lost on me, and the fun of running my own ship, albeit small, was enticing. I would take it if it were offered. The big problem was: Would Nice even reopen? We had a couple of anxious months, and then it became official: Nice would reopen as a consulate general and I would be the consul general to do the honors.

I was then in as good a shape regarding alcohol as I had been for a long time. My line to my friends was that I no longer drank—or almost never. It had become easy to ask for soda water, and to drink wine "in moderation." I would have wine at the appropriate meals, but the theory was that I would only sip and never finish my glass. That's pretty much what happened. True, I could be slow on the draw when a hostess or a waiter refilled my glass, but an extra half glass of wine at dinner was not what was going to get me into real trouble. On the important issue, secret drinking, I was doing well—better than I had in years. I had gone months with no sneaking at all. I went to Nice confident that I had enough control over alcohol to do a good job.

I was pretty much right. From the very beginning, I established that for all practical purposes, I didn't drink. That didn't mean I couldn't accept a glass of champagne as a before-dinner libation. I wasn't a barbarian—to me, moderate drinking remained a sign of civilized living. But I tried not to drink more than a third of it. At dinner, I headed off refills of my wine glasses—often there were multiple glasses—and I left many barely touched glasses on the table. I drank no spirits. Most importantly, I did no secret tippling—well, almost none. Every once in a while, I would treat myself to *un vin blanc* at a *zinc*. It is remarkable how guilty it made me feel. But I had no little bottles squirreled away anywhere. The levels in the bottles in our liquor cabinet did not mysteriously drop. For the first time in years, I would regularly arrive at work sober.

How had I turned this corner? There can be no doubt that my chipping away at the problem, at AA, and on my own over the past few years, was beginning to pay off. It would be hard for anyone in my position not to realize that if I didn't bring my drinking under some kind of restraint, I would lose everything: my profession, my health, my wife, my family, and my friends. If the State Department got an inkling of what was going on, I could lose my job. If Louisa saw me backsliding, my marriage would be at risk. It is hard to overemphasize the importance of my relationship with Louisa. I was very aware of how blessed I was that she had stuck with me through the worst part of the drinking nightmare and how much I loved her for that—and just in general. But the risk of losing Louisa's love had been there for years and had not slowed me down. Why now, at last?

One reason I was more reliable was surely the groundwork that had been laid at AA in the past years. I had been making progress, becoming more reliable, and having fewer slips. Despite the occasional slips, I was feeling more confident than I had for a long time.

Nevertheless, it is clear that some of my improvement in Nice had to do with the nature of the job. Being the American consul general in Nice was small potatoes, but you would never know it by counting the perks I received. We were ensconced in a house fit for a movie set, with a wide terrace overlooking a pool and an utterly picture postcard view of the harbor of Villefranche and Cap Ferrat beyond. We were given a live-in domestic staff of two, not counting either the gardener or the chauffeur—or his backup. That's just for starters.

We also had heavy security. There had been five attacks on senior U.S. Foreign Service officers in France in the previous two years, including one on the consul general in Strasbourg who had been shot five times, yet survived. Therefore, senior U.S. diplomats in France, which included all five consuls general, were given special protection. In

Nice, this was accomplished by a van parked at the entrance of our residence, staffed 24/7 by armed, uniformed French guards. Moreover, my official vehicle was a bulletproof stretch limo. In theory, I was to go nowhere except in that car, always driven by one of the chauffeurs, both of whom had special training in attack avoidance. Louisa and I of course cheated a bit, and would beetle around the coast alone on weekends in our little red Toyota Tercel. I told her that if we were killed on one of those outings, the embassy would be very cross.

The visibility of the U.S. consul general in Nice was also heightened by the fact that both the mayor of Nice and, more especially, the prince of Monaco wanted to play up the importance of the American diplomatic presence. (The little principality of Monaco fell within my sphere, and I was the only American diplomat accredited to it.) Prince Rainier let it be known that he would appreciate it if when I was driving in Monaco I would always fly the American flags on my limo's front bumpers. He would schedule our appointments at times corresponding to the changing of the guard in front of the palace, so that the tourists observing that ceremony would see a flashy limo flying American flags glide up, and an authoritative-looking man in a blue suit and carrying an attaché case get out and enter the impressive portals, clearly bent on state affairs of the utmost importance.

As a result, the American consul general became a known figure in Nice—what the French call *une person-nalité*. I will never again see so many newspaper photos of myself standing around doing nothing. This exposure may be more important than meets the eye. It had the positive effect of making me cautious. I could no longer count on being anonymous, as I could in Washington. If I was out at lunch at any sort of official function, I was at the head table. If I ate alone in a restaurant, I could count on people stopping to say hello. I became a more prudent man.

Of course, my alcohol record was not perfect. Louisa was away from time to time, sometimes to serve as a master teacher at the Folger Shakespeare Library in Washington. When she was away I wasn't very bad; but it was summer, a time to let everything get a little lax. Pierre, the chef, took to wearing shorts and flowered shirts, and Kiki, his Tahitian wife, stopped wearing shoes, stayed in her sarong to serve dinner, and was never without a hibiscus bloom behind her ear. In times such as these, who could fault a guy for having a second glass of wine at lunch or even for taking a little break at about four in the afternoon to walk around the corner to that nice little bistro where he hardly ever went, and might not even be known, for a little mid-afternoon glass of muscadet?

The irony was that while I did look forward to brief periods in an empty house when I could occasionally drink too much in private, I only needed—wanted—a short time in an empty house before I badly wanted my family whole again.

Guests streamed through the house, even without Louisa there. The one incident I particularly remember— and regret—was when our daughter Eliza was in residence and an old college chum stopped by for a night. I reverted to Spee Club behavior and tied one on at dinner. It was obvious to Eliza that I had fallen off the wagon. I still wish that hadn't happened.

But for the most part, I kept well within bounds, and stayed sober.

Things were going well. Foreign service activities— economic, consular, political, and administrative—are divided into those four cones. I have mentioned that the political cone is thought to be the home of the Foreign Service elite, and that's where all my experience was, but I found consular work extremely rewarding and would have been pleased to have done more of it over my career. People come to the consulate with problems. Consular officers can react in several ways. They can try hard to help. They can drag their feet. Or they can do something in between. In the consulate at Nice I inherited a strong can-do attitude. For this I must give credit to my extremely capable senior foreign national employee, Janet Ruiz. She was English and had been with the consulate before it closed.

She stayed on during the period it was operated as a consular agency. In this period, the activities that required an American consular officer were handled by an officer who came over from Marseille on a fixed schedule.

Janet was invaluable. It was she who had the expertise to handle the complicated consular issues that would come up regularly regarding passports or the doling out of various U.S. government funds. I tried every way I could to reinforce the positive attitude that had long prevailed at Nice before my arrival, but I must give credit where credit is due. Janet's and my joint unflagging effort to ensure that the office prioritized having a helpful attitude served us well. Our office was widely known as a great place to bring a problem.

I did a good job in Nice. We got much praise for the efficiency with which our operation functioned, and for the positive attitude we maintained. I received a commendation for the office's outstanding record. I think often of how things would have been if I had been sober for most of my working life.

The other side of my charge was to carry the flag. I will restrain myself and relate only enough to give you the flavor of our rich life in Nice. The Côte d'Azur is full of celebrities. One who immediately caught Louisa's eye as someone she would like to meet was Graham Greene, who lived in Cap d'Antibes, just down the coast from Nice. As I have explained, the consul general in Nice is a visible person-ality. If you can't get some mileage out of that by meeting some interesting people, you are not trying hard enough. I wrote Graham Greene a letter out of the blue, asking if we could come to see him. It was not at all clear to me what the answer would be.

The U.S. government had not always been very friendly towards Graham Greene. Some years earlier he had been denied a visa to enter the US because he had once been a member of the Communist Party of Britain. Happily, Mr. Greene decided to let bygones be bygones. He answered with a cordial note that he would be pleased to see us and we set a date. At the appointed time, he greeted us warmly and introduced us to his long-term lady friend. We had a nice chat and he very soon suggested we do away with sur-names. As we left, he invited us to come again soon and to bring some of his books for him to sign if we would like that. We of course accepted with alacrity.

Then we were in a bit of a bind. We had said we would come back with books to sign, but all we had were a couple of hard covers we had brought with us. We scurried around Nice and the surrounding villages looking in all the book-stores for his work. Happily, we found a few hardcovers and some paperbacks of his more popular titles. Added to the few titles we had brought with us, we had a presentable collection for his attention.

We saw Graham several more times during our stay, including at one little lunch we had for him which included some people we thought he would enjoy meeting. When we left, he gave us a couple of books warmly inscribed to us, including a wonderful little pamphlet called *J'Accuse* in which he detailed a conflict that a relative of his lady friend had had with Jacques Medecin, the local mayor. (Medecin was well known for his corruption and thuggery.) Graham inscribed it "from the condemned man," because Medecin had made some threats against Greene. The last contact we had was a card from the rest home in Switzerland where he died. He was a great man and we were grateful for that opportunity to get to know him.

Another literary highpoint was when Toni Morrison spent the night. She had been sent down by the United States Information Service to give some lectures, and I had written to see if she would like to stay with us. She accepted and we had a wonderful time introducing her to the coast and its literary side.

Ships from the Sixth Fleet were regular visitors to Nice, and we made good use of their visits to bring the US and France together. Our stay in Nice bridged the periods during which first Admiral Ed Martin and then Admiral Frank Kelso headed the fleet. They were both extremely helpful in inviting local officials to visit the ships privately or sometimes by hosting parties. A highlight was the visit of the battleship the U.S.S *New Jersey*. She was heading home in 1984 after a period of active duty, during which her 16-inch guns had engaged in massive shelling of Syrian forces in Lebanon. Modern warships have rather boxy lines and are not especially visually pleasing. Not so WWII battleships, of which the *New Jersey* was one. They are long, sleek vessels with graceful lines, and when the *New Jersey* anchored in the middle of the harbor of Villefranche, she stopped traffic.

We organized a luncheon party for Admiral Martin, her captain, because our porch was an outstanding spot from which to admire her. Louisa was planning a special meal with our outstanding chef, Pierre (of whom more later), when he stopped her.

"Let me be in charge of the dessert," Pierre asked.

He was a great chef and had flair. Of course Louisa said "yes."

Pierre would not reveal to us his surprise, but he was bursting with pleasure when, with a bit of fanfare, in he came from the kitchen with a cake he had made: a perfect replica of the *New Jersey,* down to the gun turrets and even the correct flags. Admiral Martin, a seasoned combat mariner, wept. He insisted on photographs of Pierre and his masterpiece from every angle.

The end of the Pierre saga was a letdown. We learned he was embezzling from us, so we had to let him go. His wife paid what he owed, something over $1,000, and she returned alone to Tahiti—with some help from Louisa. The replacement couple for Pierre and Kiki were boring. She was a tolerable chef, but dreary, and he drank.

Our association with Monaco was lively. Princess Grace—the former Grace Kelly—had died in an automobile accident by the time we arrived, and Rainier was prince. Young Albert was prince-in-waiting. Rainier ran Monaco like a good business. He saw his main job as keeping up the brand, and he did it well. He made every effort to ensure that any entertainment in Monaco could be counted on to be the best in the world. There was a circus week. If all circuses were like that, fewer circuses would be going out of business. There was a fireworks week. The fireworks were not only spectacular to look at, they were synchronized dramatically with classical music, which added anther unforgettable dimension.

Just as we made an effort to entertain local opinion makers with the Sixth Fleet and visiting celebrities, local officialdom entertained us. We attracted the attention of the regional authorities as well as those of nearby cities. One *préfet* (an official somewhat like a U.S. governor) organized a hike through the local Gorges de Verdun, followed by an "only in France" picnic with pâtés and cheeses and wines to die for. The *préfet* from the neighboring department, not to be outdone, took us on a lovely tour of the

Moustiers pottery factories followed by—guess what? Another fabulous déjeuner.

Twice a year I became a very hot property. At Thanksgiving and on the Fourth of July all the American entities on the coast—and there were many—wanted the presence of the American consul general as the centerpiece of their gala holiday observation. The indispensable Janet warned me in plenty of time that I would have to decide well in advance where and with whom I would personally carry the flag. As the invitations arrived, together we made a little schedule that seemed to cover the most important bases and the largest number of Americans. We shared our schedule with the petitioners, showing driving times, and we thought that was the end of it.

Not at all. We did not give the local authorities credit for the resources they had at their disposal, notably motorcycle escorts and even helicopters. Janet and I had determined that I could not attend both a Fourth of July cocktail gathering at the *palais* in Monaco at six and also a dinner at eight offered by the mayor of Cannes, a good two hours away by car. The local organizers came back with a plan that made it all possible. Mousieur le Consul Général could attend the event in Monaco in business attire from six to seven. At seven he would leave the palace with a police motorcycle escort, which would clear the way to the helipad. M. le Consul Général could change from his business attire to his dinner jacket in the helicopter, en route, and would be dressed for the evening when he arrived at the helipad in Cannes. Another motorcycle escort would whisk him to the dinner in plenty of time. And so it went.

There was also free time and fun and games. During Louisa's summer absences teaching in Washington, I was visited by a procession of nieces, each more beautiful than the last. In an effort to elevate my status with the guard contingent, I suggested with a wink and a nudge that perhaps not all the "nieces" on the approved visitor list we gave them were actually official nieces. Mousieur le Consul Général might also entertain some "friends" from time to time. I don't think I fooled any of the guard contingent.

## 21

## A ROUGH TRANSITION
## TO CIVILIAN LIFE

THE NICE POSTING ENDED NOT WITH A BANG BUT A whimper. It was 1986, Ronald Reagan was president, and the U.S. government was going through one of its periodic cost-cutting exercises. The State Department decided to shut down a large number of consulates and consulates general all over the world that it deemed marginal. Nice was on that list. I put up a vigorous defense of the little post I had opened with so much fanfare only three years earlier, but to no avail. Nice was to close. I drew the line at being the one to deliver the coup de grâce. I said I would stick around long enough to make my own goodbyes, but I would then skip town and let the consul general at Marseille take care of the nuts and bolts of the closing. The condemned man was granted his last wish.

It was a pity Nice had to close; it did have a role. But in the cold light of day, even I must confess that maintaining a consulate general in Nice was probably not cost-effective, certainly not with the level at which I was being spoiled, nor the accoutrements of the office.

With Nice closing, I decided to take early retirement and leave the Foreign Service. All but one of my overseas tours had been in French-speaking Western Europe, so I would never even be considered for an ambassadorial post anywhere but there. For all practical purposes, those posts were nearly all reserved for non-career political appointees—mostly heavy contributors to the political parties. I had had such a good time in Nice being my own boss that the idea of going back to Washington, where even the most insignificant memo had to be cleared by at the least a handful of bureaus in the Department, not to mention agencies throughout the U.S. government, was anathema to me. Even at another embassy, I would not have anything like the autonomy I had had in Nice. Going out again as consul general was not in the cards. Nice was an anachronism, slotted to be headed up by an officer in the "political cone"—as I had done. Most consulates general were reserved for persons in the consular cone, who had paid their dues issuing visas and passports. The Bureau of Consular Affairs jealously guarded those coveted senior positions for their own.

So I quit. I had been in the State Department for twenty-five years and had served for two years on active military duty on top of that. I argued that was enough service for a lifetime. My leaving, however, would not have been Louisa's first choice. There was much about the Foreign Service that she admired and enjoyed. She would miss being part of that world. She surely had to be worried about what I would do instead. My plans were vague and unformed. Write? I already had a project in mind: a guide to the lakes of Mount Desert, Maine. But that was all very much still in the planning stage. Teach? What did I know well enough to teach? Whatever I did, she and I both realized I would need structure, lest I succumb to temptations. Would I be able or willing to settle into another structured job? Lots of questions hung over us.

I clung to the book project. I was going to write a book about the lakes—known locally as ponds—on Mount Desert Island, where I had summered since my early teens. The island is dotted with stunning lakes, and as the son of my freshwater fishing father, I had a good leg up on knowing something about them. I had canoed and fished on nearly all of them. Even more importantly, I had always loved the island's freshwater and welcomed the idea of getting to know the lakes and streams better. This was a project I could put my heart into.

If I was going to be a writer, I would need to learn some new skills. I couldn't even type. During my long tenure in the State Department, officers had secretaries. One could dictate to them or give them either typed or handwritten drafts. I guess about half the officers typed their first drafts. The others wrote by hand or dictated. I had done both, but I became good at dictating and that's how I'd handled most of my work.

Learning to type was the least of my problems. In the year 1987, use of the home computer was catching on. It was clearly the wave of the future. As a would-be professional writer, I would have to get a computer and learn how to use it.

This was an exciting enterprise, and I was convinced that getting a personal computer would put me on the cutting edge. Most of my friends didn't have them yet. Three decades later, we are all accustomed to our powerful little laptops, but back in the eighties, computers came in three large major components. The computer itself was a large, clunky machine, about the size of a mid-sized suitcase that sat under your desk. A large screen that looked like an old fashioned TV set and a separate keyboard completed the ensemble. I acquired all this necessary equipment and remodeled my study to accommodate it. None of this was cheap, but I saw it as a necessary investment in the tools of my new trade.

Leaving the Foreign Service had reduced our income. We would have my pension—indexed to rise with inflation—which amounted to about half of my salary, and Louisa's small income from teaching. We also had income that my clever-with-money father had left me— without which I never would have considered retiring early. Still, we were clearly going to have to be more careful about our expenses. I certainly couldn't add the cost of a secretary into that mix. So I had to set myself up to be my own secretary.

Luckily, I had a next-door neighbor who was not only about two years ahead of me in computer ownership, but even more importantly, unlike me, he was technologically inclined. He steered me to a computer company called Leading Edge that made a serviceable, basic computer, and helped me get mine up and running. And it was he who encouraged me to go to their customer support at the long distance number he gave me. "Good advice and free," he assured me. Pretty soon I was ensconced in front of a big green screen, trying to puzzle out Word Perfect—the word processing software of choice then.

It's hard to conceive now, but back in those early days, there was no mouse or track pad. The only way to navigate around your screen was using the keyboard. Special keystroke combinations instructed the cursor to do things like "go the end of the line," or "go to the top of the page." A template fit over the top line of keys to help the beginner remember the intricacies of the system. It was very cumbersome, but it was the best around and used almost universally.

I dove right in. When I got stuck—which was often—I would call the infinitely patient people at the 801 area code help line. They could talk me back into business. Little by little, I got the hang of it, and perhaps more importantly, I also learned to type without looking at the keys— very much.

I remember getting our first post-computer phone bill. I marched into Louisa's study, where she was still tap, tap, tapping on her old-fashioned typewriter. (Louisa had been typing since college and she was right behind me in joining the computer revolution.) "Who in the world is your new best friend in Orem, Utah?" I demanded. "He's costing us a fortune."

"I'm innocent," she said, "I don't know, let alone call, anyone out there." I looked at the bill with a more discerning eye and recognized the helpful 801 area code. "Good advice, and free," my neighbor had said, which the advice was—but the phone calls weren't. I got a bit more careful, but I still used my friendly 801 number—for years.

Once I got established with the computer, I really had to get started on the book. But how? Where to begin? Washington is blessed with an institution called The

Writer's Center, which provides helpful workshops for aspiring authors. One of the offerings in the fall of 1986 was called "Writing the Query Letter." I signed up with alacrity. Helpfully, the final product of the class was one carefully crafted query letter using all the good advice we had been given during the course. We shared our letters around the room. After I read mine aloud, the instructor pronounced: "No doubt about it, if I were a Maine regional publisher I would sign you up in a heartbeat." That gave me the nudge I needed.

My draft letter promised as enclosures a table of contents and a couple of chapters. I wrote those necessary items, pulled everything together, and shipped packets off to three promising-looking regional publishing houses. Before the month was out, I had a book offer from the best known of them, the book arm of the iconic regional magazine, *Down East*. I was off and running.

Moreover, I wasn't drinking. I believed I was turning over a new leaf. I was going to be working with no supervision at all. I knew as a fact that if I began to introduce even moderate drinking into that situation that the alcohol use would creep up. I was determined to get my new life off to a clean start. I vowed not to use alcohol at all—and for a while I didn't.

## 22

## HEADING INTO
## THE END GAME

WORKING INDEPENDENTLY HAS NEVER BEEN MY best trick. I have always been greatly helped by short-term deadlines. If my boss told me he needed a paper by noon, I was on it. But tell me on the first of January that the paper isn't due until the 30th, and I may not start it until the 29th. My editor at Down East Books had only one deadline she cared about. She wanted a complete file of text in her hand by November 1st, 1987. Period.

I had broken the task down into a bunch of interim deadlines, but they were artificial, and I knew it. Nothing would happen if any of them slid. The upshot was that I had fallen behind. Not so far behind that I couldn't catch up if I worked hard, but enough to put pressure on myself.

This means that towards the end of August I became "unreliable," and my drinking was once again becoming an issue between Louisa and me. Only rarely that summer had my drinking resulted in behavior that would lead others to remark, "Bill's had too much to drink." But of course, they never saw me sozzled just before bedtime, something Louisa had to deal with regularly. While my drinking was pretty much confined within the family, I had sometimes crossed into territory that Louisa and I could agree was unacceptable, and the re-emergence of the drinking issue was hurtful to her and once again damaging to our relationship.

The way things stood with the book was that I had finished most of the text, but I still needed to fill in some gaps. Some field notes needed to be verified and I still had to double check some maps. The plan was that Louisa would go back to Washington to start the fall term teaching at Sidwell Friends School around August 25. I would stay in Maine alone to polish off those final details, heading down around mid-September.

This was not a good plan from a drinking perspective. With Louisa back in Washington, I began to slip back into the habits of my worst periods. I began to sip, sip, sip throughout the day. Safely home in the evening, I would begin to drink in earnest and would be pretty well gone by the time I rolled into bed after midnight. When you go to bed drunk, you wake up hungover. A drinker learns early on that the best—the only—cure for that hangover thirst and headache is a little bit of the hair of the dog. I began to rely on what I had always thought of in medical terms—a "mild bourbon solution"—with my morning coffee to set me straight.

I got some work done. I had prepared a good to-do list, and I ticked items off one by one; but I swigged regularly throughout the day from a bottle in the car. I had no colleagues to worry about. Still, I met people throughout the day, on my wanderings and in the village. So I did try to observe certain limits, but there is no doubt I had some encounters with people who could tell I had been drinking.

Louisa and I have always kept in touch by telephone when we are apart, usually with an evening call. Even though I called early, before I had begun my serious evening drinking, and even via long distance, she knew perfectly well that I was drinking too much—regularly. Our relationship became even more strained.

Her parents were still in Seal Harbor, and were their usual social selves, so there was no way they were not going to have me over for dinner at least once. Sure enough, the invitation came. "How about Thursday, six-thirty for seven?" I accepted, put it in my indispensable little red book, and watched it approach. Tuesday came and went, and Wednesday. On Thursday morning, I was acutely aware that I had to be presentable at six-thirty, but by then I was too caught up in the drinking routine to just skip it for a day. That just wasn't an option—not something I even considered.

I had a perfectly "normal" morning. I woke up hungover. I was then always waking up hungover. My usual aforementioned remedy, a very light, tall bourbon and water—barely an ounce of bourbon—quenched the thirst part of my hangover—and also took the edge off my need for alcohol.

I got into the car and did some field research, nipping on my pint of vodka, but in moderation. I knew I had to be careful. I headed home at about three in the afternoon, slotted my findings into the manuscript, had a snack, and went up for a nap. I felt OK. I set two alarms for 5:30 p.m. and lay down. The alarms worked fine; I woke up feeling that I was going to be all right. I got cleaned up—I have always cleaned up well—and went to dinner.

Louisa's parents knew that I had a problem with alcohol, but I thought it not beyond the realm of believability that they saw nothing seriously amiss. It's what I wanted to think. Not wanting to eat and run, I stuck it out until nine, when I took my leave. I felt terrible. I really wanted a drink badly. I had planned to go home directly from dinner, but I had a brainstorm. A small, not very popular restaurant in Seal Harbor was right on my route and open that night. I decided a nice little drink at the bar, one for the road, would be just the thing.

The place was nearly empty. I ordered a double vodka on the rocks—a no-nonsense drink whose sole function that night was to elevate the alcohol level in my bloodstream. The waitress brought me my drink. I waited a beat, and another, and a third. I didn't want to appear too eager. But then I raised my glass to my lips and tossed the whole thing right back in one swallow.

My body was wracked by a big shudder. That was a first for me. The light was low, so I don't know whether anyone noticed it. But I noticed. It was a big shudder. I have seen it, I believe, in the movies. A drunk takes a drink, shudders, wipes his mouth on the back of his sleeve and orders another. A small convulsion? Maybe that's what I'd had. Whatever it was, it lasted no more than a second and was over. I sat for a bit, then got the waitress's attention and ordered another double. This one I sipped slowly. Then I paid and went home. I had no premonition that anything had changed when I went to bed and fell asleep.

When I awoke in the morning, the events of the prior evening were clear in my mind. I remembered the dinner, and the vodka. I remembered the shudder. And sitting on the side of my bed, it became absolutely clear that I had to stop drinking. I had never thought that before. For all the times I had repeated the first step of Alcoholics Anonymous, "We admitted we were powerless over alcohol—that our lives had become unmanageable," I never believed it. I could admit—easily—that I was having a really hard time controlling alcohol and that my life was hard to manage; but I couldn't accept that I was "powerless." To do so would mean admitting I had to give up—really give up—all alcohol. Forever.

That "all alcohol forever" was what I had never before been prepared to accept. I had always carefully husbanded my little private reservations. I would quit drinking, I had told myself on many prior supposed morning epiphanies, when people were around, when Louisa was in residence. But I took refuge in the knowledge that I would be alone from time to time. If my drinking got a little out of hand then, it would be just a private thing. It wouldn't hurt anyone. No one would need to know. I had always clung tenaciously to that escape hatch. That morning, however, was something entirely new. Sitting on the edge of my bed, alone, I knew for a certainty that I was quitting completely and for good. Something mysterious and wonderful had happened. I did not want to drink.

In the past, making any new resolutions, even though they were tempered by my escape hatch equivocations, I had experienced a sense of loss. I was giving up something precious to me. I was losing a part of me—a defining part. Alcohol, I had always thought, was part of my charm. That morning, I understood that I had to leave that whole defining part behind. The miracle was that instead of loss, I felt a great, overwhelming relief. I did not doubt for a moment that my fledgling resolve was rock-solid. I was free!

I called Louisa and told her the good news: It was over for good. I was much too realistic to think she would believe it. She had heard it too often. It did not disappoint me that she was reserved in her acceptance of my news. She wasn't disparaging. She may not have even made the appropriate "That's good, dear," noises, and she certainly made it perfectly clear she was not sharing my elation. I did not press the point; time would tell, and we had plenty of that.

I was right. It was over. It is over. It has been over for more than thirty years.

I had gone overnight from being someone who could not reliably control his drinking (and in the short term, couldn't control it at all) to someone who simply did not want to drink. There are two parts to that statement. First, I lost, overnight, my craving for alcohol. I just didn't want it. Of course, I was hungover that morning; but miraculously, I didn't want what I knew to be the only relief—a little alcohol. This was not an intellectual choice. It wasn't me saying, "Bill, you have to stop drinking," (although I was saying that, too). The big change was somewhere deep inside my brain, telling my system it didn't want alcohol—it didn't want it ever.

My attitude toward alcohol that morning went beyond just not wanting a drink, it went all the way to aversion. The idea of taking a drink had become repugnant to me. I am reminded of my loathing for both gin and grape juice after getting drunk on Purple Jesuses at the cast party in Northeast Harbor when I was fifteen. The morning of my liberation, alcohol in all its forms repulsed me.

Sometimes, even now, I will pick up a glass of clear liquid, believing it to be my nice cold glass of soda water; I will take a deep pull on it, only to find it is someone's gin and tonic. I am repulsed. I don't want that in my body. I spit it back into the glass without swallowing. If I have already swallowed some I am upset. One fear I have is that I may have ingested enough to trigger that little click in my head that tells me the alcohol is beginning to do its magic. That's just what I don't want ever again—its magic.

My own conviction that a miracle had indeed happened and that I was a new person, freed from the thrall of alcohol forever, remained rock solid. Of course, it took Louisa a while to accept that the scourge that had plagued our marriage for so long was really gone for good. How could it be otherwise? How often had I promised it was over? That I was finished with drinking? Never again? And then in only days, sometimes weeks, or sometimes even months, I would slip, and the recovery had to start all over again. How could it be that I knew that this time was different? That this time there would be no slip. That I would never even want a sip?

This September (2018), I celebrated the thirty-second anniversary of that last drink. But my drinking years, and my release from that bondage, are ever near my own consciousness. Louisa and I are now both able to accept that the whole experience is behind us. But still sometimes, just out of the blue, I say to Louisa something to the effect of "Thank God, it's over," and I give her hand a squeeze. She knows what I mean.

Neither of us knows what happened. What was it that night that lifted that curse from me? Louisa sometimes attributes it to grace. We don't even know just what that is, but in religious terms, receiving grace is a gift that puts the recipient in a special relationship to God. You can't just ask to be in a state of grace. You work at it. Going to church and praying are all part of the path. Louisa thinks the years of cutting down, giving alcohol up for periods, going to AA meetings, talking about quitting and working at it, even though it didn't last, didn't work, were all steps on the path to my own grace. When the right moment came, she thinks, I was prepared to embrace it. She may be right.

Even though it's over, I am terribly aware of what a burden my drinking was on our marriage and our life together. Sometimes, again out of the blue, I tell Louisa how sorry I am for all those years and for what I put her through, for the years and years marred by my unconscionable behavior. I thank her for staying with me. "I loved you," she says, as if that explains it all. I also thank her for forgiving me. It's nearly impossible to believe it, but she has forgiven me. Her forgiveness has made a vast difference in our ability to move on.

She says the ability to forgive is a gift she was given, much as the freedom from addiction was given to me. She was able to turn the page, and not hold the long and painful drinking years against me. In the wedding service, you promise to stick it out through sickness and in health. Louisa rode through a long period of sickness, but she has put it behind her.

I don't try to conceal my former addiction. On the contrary, I have taken some voluntary steps to make it public. This book is the big one. But even before, for example, in my write-up for the blurb in my fiftieth reunion book at Harvard, I mentioned that I was an alcoholic, but that I had given up drinking many years ago. I wanted those of my college friends who had watched me start down the road toward a life-ruining addiction in Cambridge to know that I had, in fact, moved off that path. I wanted them to know that alcohol no longer plagued me, and hadn't for decades.

I am now eighty-six years old. I have neither had, nor miraculously wanted, a drink since that drink in Seal Harbor. I have a lot of good, sober times behind me; God willing I have many good sober years ahead. How awful it would be to still be drinking; how blissful it is to be free.

# AFTERWORD

By Louisa Newlin

A FORMER FOREIGN SERVICE COLLEAGUE TO WHOM Bill had given this memoir asked him, "Why did you write this?" "To tell the story," he answered. My own answer is: "To exorcise his demons." Writing this book was an act of atonement.

I am proud of Bill for writing it. He still feels enormous guilt over the years of secret drinking. But although he downplays this, he did, in fact, do some fine work for State, evidenced in his efficiency reports, and it is time for him to stop beating himself up. He has been sober for more than 30 years, and I am of course proud of that, too.

The same colleague, whom I will call Joe, said that the dramatic lifting of the burden of alcohol might encourage those who read the book to think that they, too, could "get away with it." Far from getting away with anything, Bill has paid the price many times over, in different kinds of coin—guilt, shame, a sense of failure, regret. All those passes at AA, all those periods of sobriety—these prepared him for grace, which he ultimately received.

Joe thinks that the story could offend Foreign Service officers whose trust he betrayed; he pointed out that Bill had security clearance and saw many "eyes only" memoranda and correspondence. Maybe the book will offend some FSOs, but I believe that, more importantly, it will be helpful to others, including non-FSOs, who have struggled with addiction. *Drunk at the State Department* deserves an audience wider than family and friends.

The Foreign Service is particularly conducive to alcoholism for two reasons: First, there are nonstop obligatory receptions at which alcohol flows freely; and secondly, officers are in unfamiliar surroundings, far from home and their usual support systems. Often, they are under constant stress from the threat of terrorism. (Even in a benign-seeming country like France, there were attacks on consuls general while we were in Nice. Bill was supposed to always ride in an armored limousine driven by a chauffeur trained in evasive driving.) The pressure to always be on your toes is nonstop. I find it significant that it was only when he had left the Foreign Service that Bill was able to quit drinking for good.

Another question, which Joe did not ask, is: "Why did Louisa stick it out for so long?" The short answer is that I always loved him, even when I most hated what he was doing. He was affectionate, generous, witty, and charming when he was sober, which he was for long stretches, though eventually those stretches became shorter. (He still is affectionate, generous, witty, and charming.) He was never violent. We had many good—great—times together. He never forgot my birthday or our anniversary, and he was fully present at family gatherings on Thanksgiving, Christmas, and Easter—he was the home decorator and Easter egg colorer. While I was driven to despair by the bad Bill, I did not want to lose the good Bill. I did not want the children to lose their father. He was a loving and concerned parent, and for a long time, the children were unaware of his drinking. For many years, *I* was unaware of the extent of the secret drinking. I did not see what I did not want to see, and so became an unwitting enabler—a word I had never heard of until things had become bad and I started reading up on alcoholism and seeing a psychiatrist.

It was not until we were in Guatemala in 1966, when we had been married eleven years, that the gravity of Bill's illness became clear. Bill did not want me to tell anyone else about it. When I finally wrote to his sister, Lucy Bell, knowing that she would not judge him and would continue to love him deeply, he was furious. "You told my sister!" he repeated angrily, and regularly. This, to him, was betrayal. My defense was that I needed to share my pain with someone else. It was too heavy to carry alone.

For a long time, I blamed myself for Bill's drinking. I thought I had spent too much time pursuing my academic goals, neglecting my husband, literally driving him to drink. My parents inadvertently contributed to this misunderstanding by saying things like, "Aunt Margie really has Uncle Pardee's drinking under control." (Pardee was my father's brother, who since his college days had been a heavy drinker.) Therapy helped me to see that no one can control someone else's drinking, and that I was not at fault. This helped, but there were still fights and tears (mine), which often ended in Bill walking out of the room.

The year following Bill's early retirement from the Foreign Service after 25 years, we moved back to Washington. Bill began work on the first edition of *The Lakes and Ponds of Mt. Desert Island*. His drinking had been pretty well managed in Nice, but without the daily structure of an office job, it got way out of control. Everyone who has lived with an addict of any kind knows that among the most destructive aspects of the condition are the denials and the lies that corrode trust. As Bill's alcoholism progressed, so did my buried anger.

From an Ann Landers column (really!) I learned about Al-Anon, a support group for family members of alcoholics, which, curiously, no therapist had ever mentioned to me. I went to several different meetings before finding one that was right for me, i.e., middle-aged and straight. I began seriously considering leaving Bill. Our sons had graduated from college, and our daughter was in her senior year. They would be able to handle our divorce. But I knew that separating would feel like one flesh being torn in two. By then, we had been married 32 years.

Then, in the fall of 1987, the miracle occurred that allowed him to stop drinking. It took more than a year before I had faith that his recovery was for good and began to trust Bill again. I realized that AA warns alcoholics that they are always "recovering," not "recovered," and I accept that—but every year, I feel more secure in Bill's sobriety. As Bill was given grace, which allowed him to stop drinking, I was given the gift of forgiveness. I rarely think about the bad old days. Reading what Bill has written has stirred up painful memories, but most of the time, I am able to banish them quickly.

I am glad that we are growing old together and not apart. I couldn't do it without him. We celebrated our sixty-third anniversary in June, and I love him more than ever. I admire his courage in confronting his past, and his courage in confronting the disabilities and limitations of old age. I admire his adventurous spirit. His children and grandchildren love and respect him. The last thirty years have been highly productive ones for him and have included teaching, social service, writing, and even some Shakespearean acting. He has paid his dues in full.

THE END

# ACKNOWLEDGMENTS

FIRST OF ALL, THANKS TO THE MEMBERS OF THE small memoir group with whom my wife Louisa and I have been meeting for ten years, and without whom this book would not have been written: Maureen Hinkle, John Malin, and Gay Lord. Thanks to the Writer's Center in Bethesda, MD, for providing space for our meetings.

Thanks to my son Bill Newlin Jr., publisher of Four Winds Press, who supported the idea of the book from the beginning and was involved in the details of its conception and production every step of the way. The talented designer Domini Dragoone blended creativity with discipline in working through several versions of the front cover and interior to achieve an unusual and effective result. But what I most especially appreciate was the enthusiasm she brought to the project. Myriad thanks to my daughter Eliza, a journalist and a teacher of writing, who brought her remarkable gifts to help hold the story together and worked hard and patiently on successive drafts. I also enjoyed working with Philip Turner, who line edited the final manuscript, and the extraordinarily helpful copyeditor Leah Gordon, who kept the book free from undue repetition and other small flaws.

Thanks to the numerous individuals who read and commented on early drafts or who provided other kinds of support: Anne Kozak, Kaitlyn Clarke, Sophia Seidner, Barbara Meade, Avis Bohlen, Jim Lowenstein, Frances Stead Sellers, Alexander Karelis, Lucy Bell Sellers, Rives and Dickson Carroll, Peggy Luthringer, Nick Newlin, Bill Foulke, Walter Foulke, Mary Lee Stein, Mark Rosenman, and Mariluz Vasquez.

Special thanks to Tom Dowling, an enthusiastic proponent of the book from the very beginning, who (crucially) suggested the book's title.

The most important appreciation by far goes to my wife, Louisa. The near-universal reactions shared by readers of this manuscript is that while there is no hero in this tale, there is a clear heroine in Louisa. You might think that when I first mentioned an interest in writing a book about that most shameful aspect of my life—its alcoholic side—she would have balked. Why would she encourage anything dwelling on those difficult times? From the outset, she saw the redemptive side of the enterprise and gave the book her full support.

PHOTO © WALTER FOULKE

# ABOUT THE AUTHOR

WILLIAM NEWLIN SPENT 25 YEARS AS A FOREIGN Service Officer, serving in Paris, Guatemala, Brussels, and finally as Consul General in Nice, with a Washington assignment between each overseas post. He retired after Nice, figuring it would be a hard act to follow.

His post-diplomatic activities began with a book about the lakes on Mt. Desert Island, Maine, followed by some professional Shakespearean acting, and mediating in the District of Columbia court system. He settled on teaching writing as a second career.

He has a BA and an MBA from Harvard and an MA from The Fletcher School of Law and Diplomacy. His extra-curricular loves are fly-fishing and sailing. He celebrated his eightieth birthday by sailing across the Atlantic as a crew-member of a Norwegian tall ship.

He lives in Washington DC with Louisa Newlin, his wife of 63 years. They have three children and three grandchildren.

CPSIA information can be obtained
at www.ICGtesting.com
Printed in the USA
LVHW090352051019
633253LV00001B/1/P